THE —

ENCYCLOPEDIA

OF

GARDEN
PLANTS

THE
ENCYCLOPEDIA
OF
GARDEN PLANTS

KENNETH A. BECKETT

SILVERDALE BOOKS

This edition published in 2002 by
SILVERDALE BOOKS
An imprint of Bookmart Ltd
Desford Road, Enderby
Leicester LE19 4AD

This book is adapted from *The A–Z of Garden Plants*
ISBN 1-85605-706-2

Production by Omnipress, Eastbourne
Printed in Singapore

Little, Brown
An imprint of Time Warner Books UK
Brettenham House, Lancaster Place
London WC2E 7EN

Contents

Understanding Garden Plants

The Encyclopedia of Garden Plants is a fully illustrated A–Z directory intended to be used as a source of inspiration when setting out to select plants for the garden. Creating a garden can take a great deal of planning and time, with the choice of available plants wider than ever not only in the traditional nurseries and garden centres but also in homecare centres and superstores.

Selecting the correct plants for your soil conditions and site is essential in order for the plants to thrive. Thorough preparation of the area prior to planting will help to ensure a good start for all plants, followed by regular feeding and watering while the plants establish themselves. Propagation can increase the number of plants at minimum cost to the gardener.

Having a plan is a good idea before starting to design your garden. Any problem areas can be highlighted and a solution decided on before purchasing any plants. This will help to ensure a good mix of flowers, foliage and textures throughout the garden and allow for year round colour.

The book describes the different varieties of each plant and recommends the best ones. Suggestions are given for the most desirable planting positions, along with hints on suitable soil conditions, cultivation, care and propagation.

The plants are arranged alphabetically by botanical Latin name and include annuals, biennials, perennials, rock garden plants, ornamental grasses, ferns, bulbs and tubers and shrubs. Full colour pictures throughout illustrate the range of varieties for each species.

You will discover which plants are suitable for your soil and which are not; you will learn to recognize those that thrive best in a south-facing position or require shelter against a warm wall; to identify those plants which are easy or difficult to grow.

This invaluable handbook of garden plants will help you to make the correct planting decisions, avoid unsuitable and unreliable plants and focus on those plants which are the most appropriate for your garden.

A–Z OF GARDEN PLANTS

Abelia

A genus of 30 species of evergreen and deciduous shrubs from Asia and Central America, grown for their clusters of tubular, foxglove-like flowers. The leaves are small, ovate and in pairs.

CULTIVATION. Plant out in autumn and spring in well-drained soil and a sunny or partially-shaded site. Evergreens need shelter from cold winds. Propagate by cuttings with a heel from late summer to mid-autumn.

RECOMMENDED. *A. chinensis, A. floribunda, A. x grandiflora, A. schumannii, A. triflora.*

Abelia x *grandiflora* ▶

Abutilon

Grown for their pendulous, bell-shaped flowers and long-stalked, maple-like leaves, this group of about 100 evergreen shrubs comes mainly from the tropics and subtropics. Most need to be cultivated in a greenhouse environment.

CULTIVATION. Half-hardy specimens need well-drained soil and a sheltered, sunny wall. Repot annually in spring, cutting plants back hard at the same time.

RECOMMENDED. *A. darwinii, A. x milleri, A. x suntense, A.s. Thompsonii, A. vitifolium.*

◀ *Abutilon* x *suntense*

Acaena

Low-growing, mainly evergreen perennials and sub-shrubs, this group of 100 species chiefly comes from the Southern Hemisphere. They bear spiny, decorative, bur-like fruit.

CULTIVATION. They require moist, but well-drained soil and a sunny or partially shaded site. Propagate by division or from seed in spring.

RECOMMENDED. *A. buchananii, A. Blue Haze, A. caesiiglauca, A. glaucophylla, A. inermis, A. magellanica, A. microphylla, A. novae-zelandiae, A. ovalifolia, A. pusilla.*

Acaena microphylla ▶

Achillea

A hummock forming perennial with flattened, bright yellow flower heads that are popular for flower arranging. The light green, feathery leaves grow in pairs on either side of the stem.

CULTIVATION. Easy plants to grow that like stony or chalky soils. Support the stems by staking. Plant in autumn or spring in well-drained soil in sun. Propagate by division in autumn or spring. Flowering season: summer to autumn.

RECOMMENDED. *A. ageratifolia*, *A. chrysocoma*, *A. filipendulina*, *A. huteri*, *A. rupestris*.

◀ *Achillea filipendulina* Golden Plate

Aconitum

This group of tall or climbing herbaceous perennials have deep lobed leaves and hooded flowers. All parts of this plant are poisonous. Commonly known as monkshood.

CULTIVATION. Cultivate in moist soil in a sunny or partially shaded site. Mulch each spring. Propagate by division at planting time or from seed when ripe.

RECOMMENDED. *A. amplexicaule*, *A. bicolour*, *A. carmichaelii*, *A.c.* Arendsii, *A.c. wilsonii*, *A. napellus*, *A. variegatum*.

Acontium carmichaelii Arendsii

Actaea

A hardy herbaceous perennial that is ideal for shaded areas as it prefers moist soil. Clump-forming, this plant has fluffy spikes of cream flowers and white, red or black, berry-like fruit.

CULTIVATION. Easy plants to grow that like stony or chalky soils. Plant in autumn or spring in well-drained soil and a sunny location. Propagate by division in autumn or spring. Flowering season: mid-summer to early autumn.

RECOMMENDED. *A. alba*, *A. asiatica*, *A. rubra*, *A.r. neglecta*, *A. spictata*.

◀ *Actaea rubra*

Agapanthus

Evergreen or deciduous perennials with funnel-shaped, 6-sepalled flowers. They do not tolerate frost and are best planted in sheltered areas or in pots so that they can be brought into a cool greenhouse for the winter.

CULTIVATION. Plant the large tuberous roots in spring, in pots filled with a mixture of half of leaf-mould and half compost. Repot every other spring. Propagate by seed in spring.

RECOMMENDED. *A. africanus*, *A. campanulatus*, A. Headbourne Hybrid, *A. praecox*.

◀ *Agapanthus* Headbourne Hybrid

Agastache

Resembling ears of wheat, this perennial plant is found in Asia and North America. The Mexican giant is a clump-forming specimen, with red tubular flowers that form terminal spikes in summer.

CULTIVATION. Grow in any well-drained soil in a sunny location. Plant in autumn or spring. Propagate by division or from seed during the spring.

RECOMMENDED. *A. mexicana*.

Agastache mexicana ▶

Ageratum

This group are mainly annual plants from the tropical areas of America. One half-hardy annual is a popular bedding plant. The pompom-like flowers can be coloured both blue-purple and pink-white.

CULTIVATION. Plant in ordinary garden soil, enriched with a little peat or compost in full sun. Liquid feed every fortnight. Propagate from seed in spring.

RECOMMENDED. *A. houstonianum*.

◀ *Ageratum houstonianum*

Agrostemma

These annual plants can be found in both the Mediterranean and South Russia. The plants have narrow stems and bear solitary 5-petalled flowers in red-pink, lilac-pink and rose-purple colours.

CULTIVATION. These plants are happy in any well-drained soil in a sunny location. Sow seed in mid to late spring, or in mid-autumn for early flowers.

RECOMMENDED. A. *githago*, A.g. Milas.

Agrostemma githago Milas ▶

Ajuga

A group of 40 annuals and perennials from Europe and Asia. This species forms low matts or wide clumps of leaves with erect stems bearing whorls of tubular flowers.

CULTIVATION. Plant from autumn to spring in any ordinary garden soil in sun or shade. Propagate from seed or by division in spring or after flowering.

RECOMMENDED. A. *genevensis*, A. *pyramidalis*, A.p. Crispa, A. *reptans*, A.r. Purpurea, A.r. Variegata.

◀ *Ajuga reptans*

Alchemilla

A low, tufted, spreading herbaceous plant with rounded leaves and tiny, yellowish-green flowers in clusters or panicles. There are 250 species and are very easy to grow in sun or shade, in ordinary garden soil. A good ground cover specimen.

CULTIVATION. Plant in autumn or spring. Propagate by division at planting time or from seed in spring.

RECOMMENDED. A. *alpina*, A. *conjuncta*, A. *erythropoda*, A. *mollis*, A. *splendens*.

Alchemilla mollis ▶

Allium

A group of 450 mainly bulbous perennial species of 6-petalled, starry or bell-shaped flowers. This includes popular vegetables such as chives, garlic and onions and most species will smell of garlic or onion when bruised. They make very fine cut flowers with their elegant foliage. Depending on which variety is cultivated, they can grow to a height of between 15–150 cm. Plant out in fertile garden soil in a sunny or partially-shaded site.

CULTIVATION. Enrich soil with compost, if necessary, after digging over the bed thoroughly. Plant small bulbs at a depth of 5–10 cm by hand. Plant larger bulbs using a dibble so as not to damage the bulb. Carefully check each bulb for traces of rot. If any rot is detected, then treat with a fungicide powder. Most varieties can be left in the ground to encourage clumps to form. Dwarf species can be grown successfully in pots.

RECOMMENDED. *A. amabile, A. callimischon, A. campanulatum, A. cernum, A. chamaemoly, A. christophii, A. elatum, A. falcifolium, A. flavum, A. giganteum, A. mairei, A. moly, A. neapolitanum, A.n. cowanii, A. odorum, A. pulchellum, A. pyrenaicum, A. rosenbachianum, A. roseum, A. schubertii.*

▼ *Allium rosenbachianum*

▲ *Allium giganteum*

▲ *Allium neapolitanum*

Allium albopilosum ▼

A.o. ostrowskianum ▼

 ▼ *Allium moly*

Allium narcissifolium ▼

Alstroemeria

A tuberous-rooted perennial originating from South America. The flowers appear in a wide variety of colours from white to pink, yellow or orange. Ideal for the herbaceous border and a good specimen for flower arrangements.

CULTIVATION. Grow in well-drained soil in a sheltered, sunny site; tender species need protection from frosts. Leave undisturbed to form clumps. Propagate by division or seed in spring.

RECOMMENDED. *A. brasiliensis*, *A. gayana*, *A. hookeri*, A. Ligtu hybrids, *A pulchella*.

Alstroemeria Ligtu hybrids

Althaea

A genus of 12 species with showy, 5-petalled flowers. Best positioned at the back of a border, slightly in the shade. Often considered a perennial, it can be prone to rust disease and is best treated as a biennial, raising new plants each year.

CULTIVATION. Plant in well-drained garden soil. Propagate from seed, spaced well apart, sown in early summer where plants are to flower. Treat against rust every month.

RECOMMENDED. *A. ficifolia*, *A. rosea*.

 Althaea ficifolia

Alyssum

A group of annuals, perennials and sub-shrubs that are mat or hummock-forming. The leaves are hairy, often grey or silver and the flowers are bright yellow and 4-petalled. An easy to grow plant.

CULTIVATION. Grow from seed in trays and plant out in a sunny, well-drained location. Protect young plants from slugs and snails.

RECOMMENDED. *A. argenteum*, *A. folium*, *A montanum*, *A. saxatile*, *A.s.* Citrinum, *A.s.* Plenum, *A. spinosum*, *A. troodii*.

Alyssum spinosum Roseum

Amaranthus

The flower clusters of some of this species droop in crimson, catkin-like tassels. Other species have erect flower stalks or ball-like clusters. Considered half-hardy, this plant can be grown in any well-drained soil, preferably enriched with compost.

CULTIVATION. Raise from seed sown under glass in spring. Plant out mature seedlings when all danger of frost has passed.

RECOMMENDED. A. *caudatus*, A. *gangeticus*, A. *tricolour*, A.t. Joseph's Coat, A.t. Molten Fire.

◀ *Amaranthus tricolour* Joseph's Coat

Amaryllis

A bulbous species that produces scented, trumpet-like flowers in spring, followed later by foliage. This is a plant that requires a sheltered, sunny site, preferably at the base of a wall in well-drained soil.

CULTIVATION. Plant out at the beginning of autumn when the plants are dormant, to ensure a display of leaves. Choose a southerly aspect as they like the sun. Provide protection against frosts.

RECOMMENDED. A. *belladonna*.

Amaryllis belladonna

Anagallis

A group of annuals and perennials that are low-growing and have 5-petalled red, blue or white flowers. A perennial in warm regions, but further north, treat as an annual as it does not tolerate frosts.

CULTIVATION. Propagate from seed under glass, planting out when large enough or from cuttings in early spring.

RECOMMENDED. A. *arvensis*, A. *monellii*, A.m. *collina*, A. *tenella*, A.t. Kinnadoohy, A.t. Studland.

◀ *Anagallis monellii* Philipsii

Anemone

A perennial plant of over 150 species offering a wide variety of colours and heights. The smallest grow to only 15 cm while the tallest can reach 120 cm. Flowering times vary, according to species, from early in the year through to late summer. Most prefer cool, semi-shade conditions.

CULTIVATION. Plant in well-drained, moist soil in semi-shade. Propagate by division at planting time or from seed when ripe.

RECOMMENDED. *A. apennina, A. balensis, A. biflora, A. hortensis, A. multifida, A. nemorosa, A. pavonnia. A. rivularis, A. sylvestris, A. vitifolia.*

▼ *Anemone pavonnia*

▲ *Japanese anemones*

▼ *Anemone blanda*

Anemone x fulgens Annulata Grandiflora ▼

Anthemis

A mat-or cushion-forming group of 200 species with daisy-like flowers, with mainly white or yellow florets. Planted in beds and borders, rockeries and cut flower gardens.

CULTIVATION. Enrich soil with compost to ensure success. Plant autumn to spring in a sunny site in well-drained soil and keep well watered for the first year. Propagate by division at planting time or from seed in spring.

RECOMMENDED. *A. biebersteiniana*, *A. fructescens*, *A. sanctijohannis*, *A. tinctoria*, *A.t.* Grallach Gold.

Anthemis tinctoria E. C. Buxton ▶

Anthericum

A perennial, clump-forming plant of 300 species from Africa, Malagasy, Europe, E. Asia and America. They have thick, fleshy roots, grass-like leaves and starry, 6-petalled flowers.

CULTIVATION. Plant in autumn to spring. Propagate by division at planting time or from seed when ripe in spring.

RECOMMENDED. *A. algeriense*, *A. liliago*, *A. ramosum*.

◀ *Anthericum liliago*

Anthyllis

This is a group of 50 species of annuals, perennials and shrubs. Flowers are small, pea-like and can be coloured yellow, red, purple or white.

CULTIVATION. Plant hardy varieties in ordinary, well-drained soil in a sunny location. Tender varieties should be grown in a well-ventilated greenhouse in loam-based compost. Propagate by cuttings with a heel, division or from seed in spring.

RECOMMENDED. *A. barba-jovis*, *A. hermanniae*, *A.h. Compacta*, *A. montana*, *A. vulneraria*.

Anthyllis montana ▶

Antirrhinum

This group of short-lived perennials are best grown as annuals. They produce prostate or erect stems with racemes of tubular flowers in a wide variety of colours. Plant in groups for best effect. Good cut flower or summer bedding plant.

CULTIVATION. Grow in well-drained soil in a sunny location. Seed can be sewn directly in the soil late summer for spring flowering or in pots for winter colour.

RECOMMENDED. A. *hispanicum*, A. *majus*, A.m. Tetra Snaps, A.m. Tom Thumb, A. *semperivirens*.

Antirrhinum dwarf bedding form ▶

Aponogeton

An aquatic perennial with floating leaves and spikes of small flowers above the water.

CULTIVATION. Grow tender species in tanks in pots of loam based compost in water warmed to at least 15°C in good light. Hardy sorts can be planted in ponds or slow streams in natural mud or baskets of loam and decayed manure. Plant in the spring. Propagate by division at planting time.

RECOMMENDED. A. *distachyos*, A. *fenestralis*, A. *kraussianus*.

◀ *Aponogeton distachyos*

Aquilegia

This is a tufted or clump-forming species with nodding flowers, each having five petaloid sepals and five spurred petals. There are approximately 100 species.

CULTIVATION. Requires a well-drained, humus-rich soil in partial shade or sun. Plant out in autumn to spring. Propagate by division in spring or from seed when ripe.

RECOMMENDED. A. *alpina*, A. *bertolonii*, A. *caerulea*, A. *clematiflora*, A. *flabellata*, A. *formosa*, A. *longissima*, A. *scopulorum*, A. *vulgaris*.

Aquilegia vulgaris ▶

 *Aquilegia* x *hybrid*   *Aquilegia canadensis* ▶

▼ *Aquilegia fragrans*

▲ *Arctosis* species

Arctosis

A group of annuals, perennials and sub-shrubs with large, solitary, daisy-like flowers in shades of white, yellow, orange, red and purple. The leaves are often cut or lobed.

CULTIVATION. Grow in well-drained soil in a sunny, sheltered site. Tender varieties will need protection from frosts either with a cloche or lifted, potted and put in a greenhouse for the winter. Propagate from seed in spring or cuttings taken in late summer.

RECOMMENDED. A. acaulis, A. breviscarpa, A. fastuosa, A. stoechadifolia, A.s. grandis.

Arctosis stoechadifolia grandis ▲

Arenaria

A group of annuals and perennials that form small, tufted, creeping or mat-forming plants with 5-petalled flowers. Mostly white flowers, although occasionally pink.

CULTIVATION. Grow in well-drained sandy or gritty soil in a sunny site. Plant autumn to spring. Propagate by division or sow from seed in spring.

RECOMMENDED. A. balearica, A. ledebouriana, A. nevadensis, A. norvegica, A. purpurascens, A. tetraquetra.

 Arenaria ledebouriana

Argemone

Generally robust plants with prickly leaves and poppy-like flowers with 4–6 petals. Perennials are not reliably hardy and are best grown as annuals.

CULTIVATION. Grow in well-drained soil in a sunny, sheltered site. Sow seed *in situ* late spring or raise under glass earlier before potting on in small pots. Perennials are not reliably hardy and are best grown as annuals.

RECOMMENDED. A. *mexicana*, A. *munita*.

Argemone munita ▶

Arisaema

A species of either tuberous or rhizomatous perennials, resembling the arum plant. Each plant generally has one or two long, stalked leaves, and spikes of flowers on a fleshy stem.

CULTIVATION. Grow in a sheltered, shaded site in humus-rich soil. Tender varieties will need a greenhouse with minimum temperature of 10°C. Plant in autumn in alkaline-free compost.

RECOMMENDED. A. *candidissimum*, A. *dracontium*, A. *flavum*, A. *griffithii*, A. *robustum*, A. *speciosum*, A. *thunbergii*, A. *triphyllum*.

◀ *Arisaema candidissimum*

Armeria

Cushion or mat-forming perennials from the sea coasts and mountains with linear or grassy grey-green or silver leaves and small, 5-petalled flowers in dense, spherical heads. Some species have aromatic fern-like, foliage.

CULTIVATION. Grow in well-drained soil in a sunny site. Plant autumn to spring. Propagate by division at planting time, cuttings taken in late summer or seed sown in spring.

RECOMMENDED. A. *alliacea*, A. *juniperifolia*, A.j. Beechwood, A. *maritima*, A.m. Corsica.

Armeria maritima ▶

Arnebia

A group of 25 species, but only one species is generally available; A. echioides. The leaves are hairy and rough. The flowers are in spike-like cymes, funnel-shaped, with 5 rounded, primrose-yellow lobes, each with a black spot that fades as the flower ages.

CULTIVATION. Grow in well-drained soil in a sunny site. Plant in autumn or spring. Propagate from seed in spring, cuttings in winter or stem cuttings with a heel, late summer.

RECOMMENDED. A. echioides.

Arnebia echioides

Arnica

Although there are 25 species known, only one is generally available; A. montana. The leaves are aromatic and hairy. Flowers are generally solitary, daisy-like and an orange-red colour in late spring to summer.

CULTIVATION. Grow in any humus-rich soil in a sunny site. Plant autumn to spring. Propagate by division or from seed in spring.

RECOMMENDED. A. montana.

 Arnica montana

Artemisia

There are 400 species of this plant that has small leaves, finely dissected and covered in silky or woolly hairs. Flower-heads are small to very small, with tubular florets that are wind pollinated. Many of this species are aromatic and several are used as culinary herbs.

CULTIVATION. Grow in well-drained soil in a sunny site. Plant autumn to spring. Propagate by cuttings in late summer or by division in spring.

RECOMMENDED. A. arborescens, A. dracunculus, A. lactiflora, A. Nutans, A. stellerana.

Artemisia stellerana

Aruncus

This is a robust, clump-forming, woody-based herbaceous plant with large leaves. Flowers are very small, 5-petalled, creamy-white in dense, plume-like stems, appearing in summer.

CULTIVATION. Grow in moisture retentive soil in partial shade or sun. Plant autumn to spring. Propagate by division at planting time. Seed may be sown in spring, but is slow to reach maturity.

RECOMMENDED. A. *dioicus*, A.d. Kneiffi, A.d. *triternatus*.

◀ *Aruncus dioicus*

Arundinaria

This group of bamboo species originates from the warmer regions of the world. Clump-forming, with narrow, oblong leaves, some species spread by rhizomes. Grass-like flowers are rarely produced, often hidden by the leaves.

CULTIVATION. Grow the hardy species in moisture-retentive soil in partial shade or sun, sheltered from strong, cold winds. Plant and propagate by division in spring.

RECOMMENDED. A. *anceps*, A. *japonica*, A. *murielae*, A. *nitida*, A. *simonii*, A. *viridistriata*.

Arundinaria viridistriata ▶

Asperula

Mainly small plants, this species are tufted to mat-forming, with square stems, narrow leaves in whorls and slender, tubular flowers with 4 lobes.

CULTIVATION. Grow in well-drained soil in sun. Some species prefer alpine conditions with gritty soil. Plant autumn to spring. Propagate from seed, by division in spring or cuttings in summer.

RECOMMENDED. A. *arcadiensis*, A. *gussonii*, A. *lilaciflora caespiosa*, A. *nitida*, A. *orientalis*, A. *suberosa*.

◀ *Asperula suberosa*

Aster

This is a group of mainly hardy, herbaceous perennials. Generally clump-forming with erect stems with terminal clusters of daisy-like, star-shaped, flower-heads and narrow leaves. They bloom from the begininning of summer through to winter. A robust specimen that can adapt to poor soils.

CULTIVATION. Plant in summer or spring in any ordinary soil that does not dry out excessively, in sun or partial shade. Mulch the soil in summer and water in hot weather. This will help prevent any attacks of oidium that appears as felty white patches on the leaves. Treat with triforine. Divide plants every three years, in spring, to maintain a good display of flowers and replant cuttings in a new, fresh location in rich soil.

RECOMMENDED. A. alpinus, A. amellus, A. cordifolius, A. ericoides, A. farreri, A. x frikartii, A. laterifolius, A. novae-angliae, A. novi-belgii, a. tradescantii.

▼ Aster x frikartii

Aster ericoides ▼

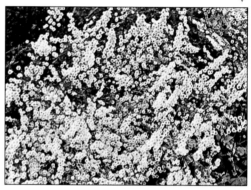

▼ Aster cordifolius Silver Spray

Aster novi-belgii

Aster alpinus

Aster novae-angliae Harrington's Pink

Aster amellus King George

Aster amellus King George

Aster novi-belgii

Astilbe

A herbaceous perennial with clump-forming habit or rhizomatous plants with plume-like 4–5 petalled flowers rising from fern-like foliage.

CULTIVATION. Grow in moist soil, preferably near a stream or pond, in sun or shade. Plant in autumn to spring. Propagate by division at planting time or from seed in spring, which can be very slow.

RECOMMENDED. A. x *arendsii*, A. *chinensis*, A.c. *davidii*, A. x c. Peter Pan, A. *grandis*, A. *japonica*, A.j. *terrestris*, A. *microphylla*, A. *simplicifolia*.

Astilbe x *arendsii* ▶

Aubrieta

A mountain species of 15 evergreen, trailing or mat-forming perennials. Colours vary from red to purple, pale and deep blue through to mauve. Often planted to grow over walls or border steps.

CULTIVATION. Plant in winter with a handful of sand around the base to avoid rot. After flowering, clip off all the dead heads to encourage the foliage to thicken out. Propagate by seed or by division in spring.

RECOMMENDED. A. *deltoidea*, A.d. Dr Mules, A.d. Leichtlinii, A.d. Red Carpet, A.d. Wanda.

◀ *Aubrieta deltoidea*

Aucuba

A genus of 3–4 evergreen shrubs. They have insignificant 4-petalled flowers. In female plants the flowers are followed by glossy, red fruit. Male and female plants must be grown together if fruit is required.

CULTIVATION. Grow in any moisture-retentive, but well-drained soil in shade or partial shade. Plant autumn to spring. Propagate from seed when ripe or by cuttings late summer, autumn.

RECOMMENDED. A. *chinensis*, A. *japonica*, A.j. Gold Dust, A.j. Longifolia, A.j. Speckles, A.j. Varieagata Maculata.

Aucuba japonica ▶

Begonia

A moderately hardy genus of 900 species with lopsided, ear-shaped leaves and clusters of 4–5 petalled flowers.

CULTIVATION. Most species require greenhouse treatment, a minimum temperature of 7–10°C and shade from direct sun. Grow in any commercial potting mixture and liquid feed through the summer. Propagate by stem or leaf cuttings in spring or from seed in late winter or early spring.

RECOMMENDED. *B. evansiana*, *B. semperflorens*, *B. sutherlandii*, *B.*x *tuberhybrida*.

 Begonia x *tuberhybrida* Pendula

Belamcanda

One of a genus of 2 species, one of which is generally available. This plant has leaves that are iris-like and sword-shaped and bears orange-red, purple-brown spotted flowers in summer followed by a shining, black, seed capsule.

CULTIVATION. Grow in well-drained, humusrich soil in a sheltered, sunny or partially shaded site with protection from severe frosts. Plant in spring. Propagate by division or from seed in spring.

RECOMMENDED. *B. chinensis*.

Belamcanda chinensis

Bellis

A low-growing, clump-forming perennial plant with either single or double, pompom shaped, daisy flower-heads and spoon-shaped leaves.

CULTIVATION. Grow in ordinary garden soil in sun or partial shade. Plant late autumn to early spring. Propagate by division at planting time or from seed in spring.

RECOMMENDED. *B. perennis*, *B. sylvestris*.

Bellis perennis

Berberis

This group of 450 species of evergreen or deciduous shrubs, the main characteristic of which is the system of long and short shoots. The bowl-shaped flowers are yellow, orange or reddish in colour. The fruit is coloured pinky-red and black-purple and can sometimes be covered in a waxy patina. Mostly the species are hardy except where the frosts are severe.

CULTIVATION. Tender varieties need a warm, sheltered, site or a frost-free greenhouse. All species need well-drained soil in sun or light shade. Plant autumn to spring. Propagate by cuttings with a heel in late summer, or from seed sown when ripe. Well-suckered specimens can also be divided successfully.

RECOMMENDED. *B. aggregata, B. buxifolia, B. candidula, B. x c. Barbarossa, B. carminea, B. darwinii, B. gagnepainii, B. hookeri, B.h. viridis, B. jamesiana, B. julianiae, B. linearifolia, B. polyantha, B. pruinosa, B. sargentiana, B. thunbergii, B. verruculosa, B. vulgaris, B. wilsoniae, B.w. subcaulialata.*

▼ *Berberis* x *stenophylla*

▲ *Berberis darwinii* in fruit

▲ *Berberis darwinii*

▲ *Berberis linerifolia* Orange King

Berberis wilsoniae in fruit ▼

Berberis thunbergii Rose Glow ▼

Bergenia

Evergreen perennials with stout, semi-woody rhizomes, rounded, leathery leaves and bell-shaped flowers of 5 or more petals. These plants make good ground cover beneath trees.

CULTIVATION. Grow in humus-rich soil in partial shade, sheltered from strong winds. Plant autumn to spring. Propagate by division at planting time or from seed in spring.

RECOMMENDED. B. Abendglut, B. ciliata, B. cordifolia, B. crassifolia, B. delavayi, B. purpurascens, B. x schmidtii, B. stracheyi, B.s. Alba.

◀ *Bergenia cilicata ligulatas*

Bletilla

A group of 9 orchids from East Asia. The stems are wiry with pleated leaves. The flowers can be rose-purple or white tinged with rose.

CULTIVATION. A hardy, clump-forming species suitable for sheltered sites in sun or partial shade. Can also be grown in pots of peaty soil in a cold greenhouse. Repot and divide when necessary. Propagate by division after flowering, or in spring.

RECOMMENDED. B. striata, B. striata Alba.

Bletilla striata

Boykinia

A group of clump-forming to spreading plants with kidney-shaped leaves and small, bell-shaped flowers with 5-petal clusters.

CULTIVATION. Grow in humus-rich, moisture-retentive soil in partial shade or sun. Plant autumn to spring. Propagate from seed when ripe, or division after flowering or in spring.

RECOMMENDED. B. aconitifolia, B. jamesii, B. tellomoides, B.t. watenabei.

◀ *Boykinia jamesii*

Brachycome

The perennials in this group have mainly tufted growth, while the annuals are erect and branched. The flower heads are daisy-like.

CULTIVATION. Grow in well-drained soil in sun. Plant perennials in the autumn or spring. Sow half-hardy annuals seed in spring and plant out when all danger of frost has passed. Propagate perennials by division or seed in spring.

RECOMMENDED. B. iberidifolia, B. nivalis, B. rigidula.

Brachycome iberidifolia ▶

Brizia

A genus of 20 annuals and perennials. Tufted plants with natural and perennials grasses with narrow leaves and spikelets of helmet-shaped flowers.

CULTIVATION. Grow in well-drained, fertile soil in a sunny site. Sow seeds of annuals *in situ* in autumn or spring. Plant and propagate perennials from seed or by division in spring.

RECOMMENDED. B. maxima, B. media, B. minor.

◀ *Brizia maxima*

Brunnera

A genus of 3 herbaceous perennials. One species is readily available, B. macrophylla. A clump-forming plant with heart-shaped leaves. Long stalks of flowering stems bear forget-me-not-like flowers in spring, summer and again in autumn. The variegated form has creamy-white margins on its leaves.

CULTIVATION. Grow in moist soil in sun or shade. Plant autumn to spring. Propagate by division in spring.

RECOMMENDED. B. macrophylla, B.m. Variegata.

Brunnera macrophylla Variegata ▶

Buddleia

Also known as the butterfly bush because its scent is very attractive to butterflies. This group of deciduous and evergreen shrubs have small, tubular flowers of 4 petals. In some varieties, the flowers are followed by berries. The fragrant flowers are borne on arching stems in conical clusters from summer to autumn. Hardy species require well-drained soil in a sunny site. Tender varieties need a frost-free area or a greenhouse with minimum temperature of 7°C.

CULTIVATION. Plant out or pot autumn to spring. Propagate by cuttings, preferably with a heel in late summer. To prevent self-seeding, cut spent flower-heads back to a pair of sideshoots. This may result in a second flowering. In late autumn or spring, remove the previous season's flowering heads and cut off several centimetres of stem. Hard pruning each spring will keep this plant in a compact size for a small garden.

RECOMMENDED. B. *alternifolia*, B.*a*. Argentea, B. *asiatica*, B. *auriculata*, B. *colvilei*, B. *crispa*, B. *davidii*, B.*d*. Black Night, B.*d*. Harlequin, B.*d*. White Profusion, B.*d. fallowiana*, B. *fallowiana*, B.*f*. Alba, B. *globosa*, B.*g*. Lemon Ball, B. x Lochinch, B. x *weyeriana*.

▼ *Buddleia alternifolia*

Buphthalmum

There are six species of these herbaceous perennials from Europe. They are clump-forming plants with showy, daisy-like flower-heads.

CULTIVATION. Grow in any humus-rich moisture retentive soil in sun or partial shade. Plant out autumn to spring. Propagate from seed or by division in spring.

RECOMMENDED. B. salicifolium, B. speciosum.

Buphthalmum speciosum

Bupleurum

There are 150 species of annuals, perennial and shrubs in this group. The leaves are distinguished by parallel veins and the flowers are tiny, 5-petalled, greenish-yellow, white or purple

CULTIVATION. Grow in any well-drained soil in a sunny site. Plant autumn to spring. Propagate from seed in spring, division of perennials autumn to spring, or cuttings with a heel in spring.

RECOMMENDED. B. angulosum, B. falcatum, B. fruticosum.

Bupleurum fruticosum

Buxus

A hardy herbaceous perennial that is ideal for shaded areas as it prefers moist soil. Clump-forming, this plant has fluffy spikes of cream flowers and white, red or black, berry-like fruit.

CULTIVATION. Easy plants to grow that like stony or chalky soils. Plant in autumn or spring in well-drained soil and a sunny location. Propagate by division in autumn or spring. Flowering season: mid -ummer to early autumn.

RECOMMENDED. B. balearica, B. harlandii, B. japonica, B. microphylla, B. sempervirens.

Buxus sempervirens

Calandrinia

A mainly low-growing, clump-forming, species with bowl-shaped, 5–7 petalled flowers in shades of pink to red-purple that thrive in the sun. This half-hardy species is mostly grown as a annual.

CULTIVATION. Grow in well-drained soil in a sheltered, sunny spot. Seed should be sewn in spring at a temperature of 15–18°C. Plant out when all danger of frosts has passed.

RECOMMENDED. *C. discolour, C. crassifolia, C. umbellata.*

◀ *Calandrinia umbellata*

Calceolaria

A group of 300 annuals, perennials and shrubs with unusual pouch-like flowers, which explains the common name of slipper plant or slipper wort. Some species are hardy, such as the alpine variety. Others need greenhouse conditions.

CULTIVATION. Plant the hardy sorts in well-drained, moist soil in sun or partial shade. Grow tender species in pots under glass. Seed should be sewn in a cool greenhouse or frame in mid-summer. Alpines are propagated from seed or division in spring. Provide protection from slugs.

RECOMMENDED. *C. acutifolia, C. arachnoidea, C. bicolour, C. biflora, C. darwinii, C. falklandica, C. fothergillii, C. herbeohybrida, C. intergrifolia, C.* x John Innes, *C. mexicana, C. polyrrhiza, C. scabiosifolia, C. tennella.*

▼ *Calceolaria x herbeohybrida*

Calceolaria integrifolia ▼

Calendula

Popular annual bedding plants and cut flowers, with yellow or orange, daisy-like flower-heads. Regular dead-heading will extend the flowering time. Varieties can be single or double flowered. They seed themselves very easily and are robust plants.

CULTIVATION. An easy to grow species. Grow in any well-drained soil in a sunny site. Sow seed *in situ* in spring or autumn.

RECOMMENDED. *C. arvensis*, *C. officinalis*.

Calendula officinalis Radio ▶

Callicarpa

This group of deciduous shrubs have 4-lobed, tubular flowers and small, rounded, berry-like fruit. The large leaves are pale green in colour.

CULTIVATION. Grow in any well-drained, humus-rich soil in a sheltered, sunny site against a hedge or wall. Sow seed *in situ* in spring or autumn. Plant autumn or spring. Propagate by cuttings late summer or from seed when ripe.

RECOMMENDED. *C. bodinieri*, *C. dichotoma*, *C. japonica*, *C.j. leucocarpa*.

◀ *Callicarpa bodinieri*

Callistephus

A half-hardy annual from China and Japan. Species are classified according to their flower-head shape; Ball, Chrysanthemum-flowered, Ostrich Plume, Peony-flowered, Pompom, Spider. Varieties come in shades of red, purple and white. There are also some bicoloured varieties.

CULTIVATION. Grow in well-drained, humus-rich soil in a sunny site. Sow seed under glass. Plant out autumn to spring when all danger of frost has passed.

RECOMMENDED. *C. chinensis*.

Callistephus Fire Devil ▶

Calluna

A very variable species of low, evergreen shrubs commonly known as heather. Easily recognised by the vertical spikes of flowers that appear late summer through to winter.

CULTIVATION. Grow in an acid, preferably peaty soil in a sunny site. Some shade can be tolerated. Propagate by cuttings taken with a heel in late summer. A light shearing after flowering will keep plants bushy and promote future flowering.

RECOMMENDED. *C. vulgaris*, *C.v.* Alba Elata, *C.v. hirsuta*.

Calluna vulgaris H. E. Beale ▶

Caltha

Herbaceous perennials with a clump-forming habit and cup-shaped flowers, formed of 5 or more petals in shades of yellow or white.

CULTIVATION. Grow bog species in wet ground or by the waterside; alpines should be grown in gritty but moist soil, both in a sunny site. Plant autumn to spring. Propagate by division in spring, after flowering or from seed.

RECOMMENDED. *C. howellii*, *C. introloba*, *C. leptosepala*, *C. minor*, *C. palustris*, *C. polypetala*.

◀ *Caltha palustris*

Calycanthus

Deciduous, aromatic shrubs with oval leaves, terminal flowers and urn-shaped fruit from America. Some varieties have fragrant flowers and the colours range from crimson-brown to reddish-purple.

CULTIVATION. Grow in any well-drained soil in a sunny site. Plant autumn to spring. Propagate from seed when ripe or in spring or by layering in spring or autumn.

RECOMMENDED. *C. fertilis*, *C. floridus*, *C. occidentalis*.

Calycanthus floridus ▶

Camellia

An evergreen species of shrubs and trees with leathery leaves and rose-like flowers. Only suitable for neutral to acid soil. Good pot plants for the cool greenhouse or room.

CULTIVATION. Hardier species can be grown on a sheltered wall in partial shade or in a frost-free greenhouse. Plant in autumn or spring. Propagate by stem or leaf-bud cuttings in late summer.

RECOMMENDED. *C. auspidata, C. japonica, C.j. Snowflake, C. reticulata, C.r. Crimson Robe, C. saluenensis, C. sinensis, C. x williamsii.*

◀ *Camellia* Inspiration

Campanula

Most of this species are herbaceous perennials, many of a dwarf stature and suitable for rock gardens, beds or borders. The foliage varies and the flowers range from wide, open stars to tubular bells in shades of blue, pale yellow and white. Most are hardy.

CULTIVATION. Grow in well-drained soil in sun or light shade. Plant autumn to spring. Propagate from seed, division at planting time or from cuttings taken in late spring.

RECOMMENDED. *C. alliariifolia, C. carpatica, C. cohearifolia, C. glomerata, C. latifolia, C. medium, C. muralis, C. persicifolia, C. poscharskyana, C. sarmatica, C. takesimana, C. trachelium.*

▲ *Campanula persicifolia* Alba

Campanula poscharskyana ▼

▼ *Campanula isophylla* Star of Italy

Campsis

Deciduous, woody climbers with aerial roots. and clusters of flowers with 5, rounded, petal-like lobes. Grown on sunny walls or over dead tree stumps.

CULTIVATION. Grow in well-drained, moisture retentive, humus-rich soil. Plant autumn to spring. Propagate from seed, layering or suckers in spring or cuttings with a heel late summer.

RECOMMENDED. C. *grandiflora*, C. *radicans*, C. x *tagliabuana*.

◀ *Campsis grandiflora*

Cardiocrinum

Resembling lilies, this species of bulbous plants requires similar growing conditions; partial shade and shelter from strong winds.

CULTIVATION. Grow in a moist, humus-rich soil in a sheltered site. Plant in autumn, setting the bulb shallowly and only just covered with soil. Propagate by separating at planting time the small bulbs that form around the base of the flowering specimens. Seedlings take 6–8 years to reach flowering size.

RECOMMENDED. C. *cordatum*, C. *giganteum*.

Cardiocrinum giganteum

Carex

A species of sedges, mainly from wet soils and temperate climates. They are spreading plants, with arching leaves and slender flowering stems. The tiny, greenish or brownish, petalless flowers are arranged in dense, short, catkin-like spikes.

CULTIVATION. Grow in a moisture-retentive soil, by water. Plant spring or autumn. Propagate from seed or by division in spring.

RECOMMENDED. C. *brunnea*, C.b. Variegata, C. *buchanii*, C. *elata*, C.e. Aurea, C. *grayi*, C. *morrowii*, C. *ornithopoda*, C.o. Variegata, C. *pendula*.

◀ *Carex elata* Aurea

Caryopteris

A group of small, deciduous shrubs with small, 5-lobed, tubular flowers that appear late summer to autumn.

CULTIVATION. Grow in well-drained soil in a sunny location. Plant in spring. Propagate by cuttings with a heel in summer, over-wintering plants in a cold frame or greenhouse. Cut back previous season's growth to maintain flowering.

RECOMMENDED. *C.* x *clandonensis*, *C.* x *c.* Arthur Simmonds, *C.* x *c.* Kew Blue, *C. mongholica*.

Caryopteris x *clandonensis* Kew Blue ▶

Cassinia

A species of evergreen shrubs with slender stems, small leaves and clusters of tiny, daisy-like flower-heads. Considered hardy except in all but the severest of winters, when the leaves may turn brown or the plant may be killed back to ground level.

CULTIVATION. Grow in any well-drained soil in a sunny site. Plant autumn to spring. Propagate by cuttings with a heel late summer.

RECOMMENDED. *C. fulvida*, *C. leptophylla*, *C. vauvilliersii*, *C.v. albida*.

◀ *Cassinia fulvida*

Cassiope

These are very small, evergreen shrubs with tiny, densely overlapping leaves and white, bell-shaped flowers with 4–6 small lobes.

CULTIVATION. Grow in acid, peaty soil that stays moist. A cool, partially-shaded site is necessary for success. This can be a house plant in peaty compost. Plant autumn to spring. Propagate by cuttings or layering in late summer or from seed when ripe, autumn to spring.

RECOMMENDED. *C. fastigiata*, *C. hypnoides*, *C. lycopodiodes*, *C. mertensiana*, *C. tetragona*.

Cassiope x Muirhead ▶

Catananche

A genus of 5 species of annuals and perennials from the Mediterranean. They have a tufted habit with narrow, basal leaves, wiry stems and daisy-like flower-heads.

CULTIVATION. Grow in any well-drained soil in a sunny site. Avoid moist conditions or the flowers will be short lived. Plant spring or autumn. Propagate from seed in spring or root cuttings late winter.

RECOMMENDED. *C. caerulea*, *C.c.* Bicolour, *C.c.* Major.

Catananche caerulea ▶

Ceanothus

A largely evergreen species of shrubs and small trees. The tiny flowers are borne in spring, in a profusion of blue, purple, white or pink colours.

CULTIVATION. Grow in any well-drained soil in a sunny, sheltered site. Most are hardy if planted against walls, fences or in a sunny border. Some species need hard pruning each spring. Propagate by soft-tip cuttings in spring or firmer shoots with a heel in summer.

RECOMMENDED. *C. arboreus*, *C.* Burkwoodii, *C. impressus*, *C. prostratus*, *C. thyrsiflorus*.

◀ *Ceanothus* x Edinburgh

Celmisia

Evergreen perennials and sub-shrubs that have white, woollen leaves and solitary, white, daisy-like flower-heads.

CULTIVATION. Grow in well-drained, lime-free soil, preferably of large peat and granite chips. Most species will do well under scree conditions, but must not become dry at the roots. Plant in spring. Propagate from seed in spring, cuttings in spring or late summer, or by division in spring.

RECOMMENDED. *C. angustifolia*, *C, bellidioides*, *C. hectori*, *C. incana*, *C. ramulosa*, *C. sessiliflora*.

Celmisia hectori ▶

Centaurea

A very large group of annuals, perennials, sub-shrubs and shrubs of some 600 species. Varying in foliage and form, they are typified by their flowers-heads wthat are composed of several tubular florets. The bracts that enclose the heads can be notched or fringed.

CULTIVATION. Grow in well-drained soil in a sunny site. The sub-shrubby, half-hardy-to-tender types grown as summer bedding plants, need to be lifted in autumn and over-wintered in a frost-free greenhouse. Cuttings can be taken and the old plants discarded. Propagate the annuals from seed in early autumn or in spring, the perennials by division in autumn or spring and the sub-shrubs by cuttings in late summer.

RECOMMENDED. *C. cineraria, C. cyanus, C. dealbata, C. hypoleuca, C. macrocephala, C. montana, C. moschata, C. pulcherrima, C. pulchra, C.p.* Major, *C. ruthenica, C. rutifolia, C. simplicicaulis.*

▼ *Centaurea cineraria*   *Centaurea cyanus* Polka Dot ▼

◀ *C. macrocephala*   *Centaurea montana* ▲

Centranthus

A genus of annuals and perennials, but only one species is generally available; *C. ruber*. Invasive plants that seed themselves freely, they are often seen on walls in milder areas and on sea cliffs. The flowers can be red, pink or white.

CULTIVATION. Grow in ordinary, well-drained soil in a sunny site. Plant in spring or summer. Propagate from seed when ripe or by cuttings of basal shoots in late spring.

RECOMMENDED. *C. ruber (Valerian).*

   Centranthus ruber

Cephalaria

A group of 65 annuals and perennials but only one species is generally available; *C. gigantea*. This is a hardy, clump-forming perennial with dark green leaves and solitary primrose-yellow flowers in summer.

CULTIVATION. Grow in humus-rich soil in a sunny site. Plant autumn or spring. Propagate from seed when ripe or by cuttings of basal shoots in late spring.

RECOMMENDED. *C. gigantea.*

Cephalaria gigantea

Cephalotaxus

This is a group of large, evergreen, coniferous shrubs or small trees from East Asia. They have pointed leaves and plum-like fruit.

CULTIVATION. Plant in humus-rich soil in full sun or partial shade, sheltered from cold winds. Suitable for hedging as they can withstand clipping. Propagate from seed in autumn or by cuttings with a heel in late summer.

RECOMMENDED. *C. fortunei, C. harringtonia, C.h. drupacea, C.h. Fastigiata.*

   Cephalotaxus harringtonia drupacea

Cerastium

A group of mainly low-growing, mat-forming annuals and perennials. The white flowers have 5 notched petals. An invasive plant that is not suitable for the rock garden.

CULTIVATION. Grow in well-drained soil in a sunny site. Plant autumn to spring. Propagate from seed. by division in spring or by basal cuttings in spring or late summer.

RECOMMENDED. *C. alpinum lanatum, C. bieber-steinii, C. tomentosum, C.t. columnae.*

 Cerastium tomentosum

Ceratostigma

A genus of 8 species of shrubs and perennials from East Africa and Asia. These deciduous plants have a sprawling habit and are excellent ground cover specimens. The sky-blue flowers appear in autumn just before the foliage.

CULTIVATION. Grow in well-drained soil in a sheltered, sunny site. Plant in spring. Propagate the shrubs by cuttings with a heel in late summer and the well-suckered plants by division.

RECOMMENDED. *C. griffithii, C. plumbaginoides, C. willmottianum.*

Ceratostigma plumbaginoides

Cheiranthus

A group of perennials, popular as spring bedding, border or container plants. Treated as biennial, the plants are usually discarded after flowering to make way for summer bedding. Free flowering.,they have a strong scent and come in a wide range of beautiful colours.

CULTIVATION. Grow in well-drained soil in a sunny site. Plant autumn or spring. Propagate from seed sown in early summer, transferring to the flowering site in autumn.

RECOMMENDED. *C. cheiri, C. semperflorens.*

 Cheiranthus cheiri Harpur Crewe

Chelone

A group of 4 species of herbaceous perennials from East USA. They are clump-forming plants with erect stems bearing opposite pairs of leaves and terminal spikes of 2-lipped tubular flowers.

CULTIVATION. Grow in moisture-retentive, humus-rich soil in partial shade or sun; suitable for a bog garden. Plant autumn to spring. Propagate by division at planting time or from seed in spring.

RECOMMENDED. C. barbata, C. glabra, C. lyonii, C. obliqua.

Chelone obliqua ▶

Chiastophyllum

An evergreen perennial from the Caucasus Mountains, producing small mats or colonies of erect stems with rounded, fleshy, bright green leaves. The catkin-like flowers are tiny and yellowish in colour. Tolerates more shade and moisture than most succulents.

CULTIVATION. Grow in well-drained soil in sun or partial shade. Plant autumn to spring. Propagate by division in autumn or spring or by cuttings after flowering.

RECOMMENDED. C. oppositifolium.

◀ *Chiastophyllum oppositifolium*

Chimonanthus

Evergreen and deciduous shrubs with lustrous, green leaves. The flowers are bell-shaped with outer petals a dull yellow and inner petals dark red-purple, fragrant in winter. A good wall shrub.

CULTIVATION. Grow in moisture retentive, well-drained soil in a sunny site with shelter from cold winter weather. Plant autumn or spring. Propagate from seed in spring, in a cold frame or greenhouse, or layering in winter.

RECOMMENDED. C. praecox. C.p. Grandiflorus, C.p. Luteus.

Chimonanthus praecox ▶

Chionanthus

A group of deciduous shrubs with snowy-white, 4-petalled flowers in summer. The plant produces plum-like fruit but only when there is a group of plants.

CULTIVATION. Grow in moisture-retentive, humus-rich soil in a sunny site. Plant autumn to spring. Propagate from seed when ripe or layering in spring.

RECOMMENDED. *C. retusa, C. virginica.*

◀ *Chionanthus virginica*

Chionodoxa

Small, bulbous plants that produce 2–4 leaves and starry blue or blue and white flowers in early spring.

CULTIVATION. Grow in any well-drained soil in a sunny or slightly-shaded site. Plant autumn. Propagate by separating offset bulbs when dormant or from seed in autumn or spring.

RECOMMENDED. *C. gigantea, C. lucilae, C.l.* Pink Giant, *C.l.* Rosea, *C.l.* Zwanenburg, *C. sardensis, C. tmolii.*

Chionodoxa luciliae

Choisya

A group of 6 species of evergreen shrubs with one commonly grown; *C. ternata,* Mexican orange blossom. A bushy shrub with dark green leaves that emit a strong scent when bruised. The fragrant, white flowers appear in spring, but can re-appear in the autumn.

CULTIVATION. Grow in well-drained soil in a sunny site, sheltered from cold winds. Plant in spring. Propagate by cuttings with a heel late summer.

RECOMMENDED. *C. ternata.*

◀ *Choisya ternata*

Chrysanthemum

A genus of 200 species of annuals, perennials and shrubs. Some botanists consider that only the annuals are the true chrysanthemums. The flowers are often deeply dissected and the daisy-like, flowerheads come in a wide range of colours and shades, often double or semi-double.

CULTIVATION. Hardy species will grow in any well-drained, preferably humus-rich soil in a sunny site. Half-hardy plants require good, commercial potting mixture, in a well-ventilated and lightly shaded greenhouse. Propagate from seed in spring, annuals *in situ*, the perennials and shrubs under glass at 10–13°C.

RECOMMENDED. C. *alpinum*, C. *carinatum*, C. *coccineum*, C. *coronarium*, C. *coronopifolium*, C. *frutescens*, C. *leucanthemum*, C. *maximum*, C. *multicaule*, C. *nipponicum*, C. *parthenium*, C.*p.* Aureum, C. *rubellum*, C. *segetum*, C. *uliginosum*.

▼ *Chrysanthemum maximum*   *Chrysanthemum* Marjorie Boden ▼

▲ *Chrysanthemum coronarium* cultivars   *Chrysanthemum* Honeyball ▲

▲   *Chrysanthemum* Rubellum

Chrysanthemum p. Aureum   ▲

▲   *Chrysanthemum* Thora

Chrysanthemum Mason's Bronze   ▲

▲   *Chrysanthemum* Charm

Chrysanthemum Luyona   ▲

Chrysogonum

A semi-evergreen, hardy perennial that is clump-forming. The leaves are hairy and coarse whilst the flower-heads have 5, broad, golden- yellow petals, appearing in spring to autumn. Grow in any humus-rich soil in sun or shade; this plant is a sun lover, but cannot tolerate too dry conditions.

CULTIVATION. Grow in any humus-rich soil in sun or shade. Plant autumn to spring. Propagate by division at planting time.

RECOMMENDED. *C. virginianum.*

Chrysogonum virginianum ▶

Cimicifuga

A group of 15 species of herbaceous perennials. These are clump-forming plants with fluffy, small flowers, composed of up to 8 petals and numerous stamens.

CULTIVATION. Grow in humus-rich soil, preferably in partial shade, although sun is tolerated if the soil is moist. Plant autumn to spring. Propagate by division at planting time or from seed when ripe or soon afterwards.

RECOMMENDED. *C. americana, C. cordifolia, C. foetida, C. racemosa, C. simplex, C.s. ramosa.*

◀ *Cimicifuga simplex*

Cirsium

There are 150 species of annuals and perennials of this clump-forming plant. Thistle-like flower-heads are formed of slender, tubular florets, each with 5, narrow petal-lobes.

CULTIVATION. Grow in any moisture-retentive soil in a sunny site. Plant autumn to spring. Propagate by division at planting time or from seed in spring.

RECOMMENDED. *C. japonicum, C. rivulare, C.r. Atropurpureum.*

Cirsium rivulare Atropurpureum ▶

Cistus

A group of small, evergreen shrubs with 5-petalled flowers resembling roses in summer.

CULTIVATION. Grow in well-drained soil in a sheltered, sunny site. Most are hardy, but severe weather may kill the plant. Plant in spring. Propagate by cuttings taken with a heel in late summer or from seed sown in spring under glass.

RECOMMENDED. *C. clusii*, *C. crispus*, *C. ladanifer*, *C. x loretii*, *C. palhinhae*, *C. parviforus*.

 *Cistus* x *pulverulentus* Sunset

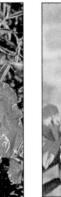

Cistus x *purpureus*

Cistus ladanifer

Cistus x *salvifolious*

Cladanthus

A group of 4 species of annuals with one being generally available. This is a bushy, aromatic plant with slender stems and daisy-like flowerheads of a golden-yellow colour. The flowers appear summer to autumn.

CULTIVATION. Grow in any well-drained soil in a sunny site, sowing seed *in situ* in spring.

RECOMMENDED. *C. arabicus*.

 Cladanthus arabicus

Clarkia

A species of 36 annuals from N .W. America and Chile. These slender, erect annual plants have flowers in terminal spikes, each with 4 petals.

CULTIVATION. Grow in any well-drained, preferably humus-rich soil in a sunny site. Sow seed *in situ* in spring or autumn in well-drained soil and a sheltered site. May also be grown as cool greenhouse pot plants.

RECOMMENDED. *C. amoena*, *C.a. whitneyi*, *C. concinna*, *C. pulchella*, *C. unguiculata*.

Clarkia pulchella

 Clarkia unguiculata

Clarkia concinna

Clematis

There are 250 species of woody and sub-shrubby climbers and herbaceous plants. The climbing species have twining stalks and tendrils. The bell-like flowers are solitary, each having 4–6 petals, while the seed is feathery and rounded.

CULTIVATION. Grow in humus-rich soil, moisture-retentive, but well-drained, ideally with the root in shade and the top in sun. The climbing species and vigorous hybrids can ramble through trees or over dead stumps and all can be grown on walls if proper supporting trellis or wire is provided. Plant autumn to spring. Propagate by stem or leaf-bud cuttings in late summer. Species clematis do not need pruning except thinning out. Cultivars such as *C. x jackmanii* are best cut back to the lowest pair of buds on each previous year's stem. This should be done in the winter and before the end of mid-spring. Pruning of other hybrids groups is optional.

RECOMMENDED. *C. alpina, C. armandii, C. flammula, C. florida, C. integrifolia, C. x jackmanii, C. lanuginosa, C. macropetala, C. montana, C. orientalis, C. paniculata, C. patens, C. recta, C. tangutica, C. texensis, C. vitalba, C. viticella.*

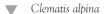 *Clematis alpina*

▼ *Clematis orientalis*   ▲ *Clematis armandii*   *Clematis Ville de Lyon* ▼

▼ *Clematis florida* Sieboldii

Cleome

A group of 150 annuals and shrubs from the tropics and subtropics. One species is widely grown; C. *hasslerana* from the West Indies. This aromatic species has white to pink flowers. Other species can be coloured pink to rose-purple and yellow.

CULTIVATION. Grow in well-drained, humus-rich soil in a sheltered, sunny site. Sow seed in spring under glass. Harden off plants in early summer and plant out after frosts have passed.

RECOMMENDED. C. *hasslerana*.

◀ *Cleome hasslerana* cultivar

Clethra

This group of deciduous and evergreen shrubs have prominent, veined leaves. They have dense, small, fragrant, 5-petalled flowers in late summer, autumn.

CULTIVATION. Grow in a sheltered, sunny or partially shaded site in a neutral to acid, humus-rich soil.

RECOMMENDED. C. *alnifolia*, C.a. Paniculata, C.a. Rosea, C. *arborea*, C. *barbinervis*.

Clethra alnifolia Rosea ▶

Cobaea

There are 18 species of these climbing plants from tropical America. One species is generally available; C. *scandens*. A woody climber with whip-like tendrils and minutely hooked tips. The flowers are bell-shaped, yellow-green changing to purple in spring through to early winter.

CULTIVATION. Can be grown as a half-hardy annual, sowing seed in mid-spring, and then planting out when all frost has passed.

RECOMMENDED. C. *scandens*.

 Cobaea scandens

Colchicum

Cormous-rooted plants, with prominently-veined leaves. The flowers are borne on a long tube that grows directly from the corm and opens into a bowl shape. Many species produce their flowers in autumn before the leaves, like some crocuses.

CULTIVATION. Grow in well-drained soil in sun. Plant late summer for autumn-flowering types, late autumn for spring bloomers. Propagate from seed when ripe or offset corms when dormant.

RECOMMENDED. *C. agrippinum*, *C. alpinum*, *C. bivonae*, *C. cilicicum*, *C. luteum*, *C. speciosum*, *C. variegatum.*

Colchicum speciosum ▶

▼ *Colchicum* Water Lily

Colchicum Lilac Wonder ▼

Coleus

This group of 150 species of perennials, annuals and sub-shrubs are grown for their brightly coloured foliage. The flowers are tubular, 2-lipped and form spike-like clusters.

CULTIVATION. Grow in good potting mixture or outdoors in summer. Propagate by cuttings in spring or late summer, from seed in spring. Usually grown as annuals, although extra large plants can be obtained by potting on into large containers each spring.

RECOMMENDED. *C. blumei*, *C.b. verschaffeltii.*

Coleus blumei hybrids ▶

Collinsia

A group of 20 species with one generally available; *C. heterophylla*. The flowers are 1–2cm in length, tubular, with the upper lip white to pale lilac, the lower lip violet to rose-purple and borne in clusters summer to autumn.

CULTIVATION. Grow in well-drained, fertile soil in a sunny or partially shaded site. Propagate from seed sown *in situ* in spring or autumn in milder areas.

RECOMMENDED. *C. heterophylla*.

◀   *Collinsia heterophylla*

Colutea

These fast-growing, summer-flowering shrubs have pea-like blooms and bladder-shaped seed pods.

CULTIVATION. Grow in well-drained soil in sun or partial shade. Each spring, prune back the bare branches to maintain a neat specimen with larger, but fewer, clusters of flowers and pods. Propagate by cuttings with a heel in late summer or from seed in spring.

RECOMMENDED. *C. arborescens*, *C.* x *media*, *C. orientalis*.

Colutea x *media*

Convallaria

An herbaceous perennial. The rhizomes creep to form dense colonies. Leaves are in twos or threes, deep green and 15–20 cm long. The bell-shaped flowers are waxy white and sweetly, strongly fragrant.

CULTIVATION. Grow in humus-rich soil in partial shade. Plant after flowering or in autumn. Propagate by division at planting time.

RECOMMENDED. *C. majalis*, *C.m.* Berlin Giant, *C.m.* Major, *C.m.* Prolificans, *C.m.* Rosea.

◀   *Convallaria majalis*

Convolvulus

A group of 250 species of annuals, perennials, sub-shrubs and shrubs. The flowers are funnel-shaped and either solitary or in small clusters.

CULTIVATION. Plant in well-drained soil in sun. The less-hardy need shelter from cold winds and frost. Plant half-hardy species in spring after frosts have passed. Propagate from seed in spring for all groups, division in spring for perennials, cuttings with a heel in late summer for shrubs.

RECOMMENDED. *C. althaeoides*, *C.a. tenuissimus*, *C. cneorum*, *C. sabatius*, *C. tricolour*.

Convolvulus cneorum ▶

Cordyline

A genus of 15 evergreen trees and shrubs with palm-like leaves. Creamy white flowers appear in mature specimens followed by berries. Often grown as a specimen plant.

CULTIVATION. Grow in well-drained soil. Pot in spring when all danger of frost has passed. Propagate from seed in spring under glass or from suckers in late spring, treating suckers as cuttings until well rooted.

RECOMMENDED. *C. australis*, *C. banksii*, *C. indivia*, *C. terminalis*.

◀ *Cordyline australis*

Coreopsis

A group of annuals and perennials with daisy-like flower-heads, popular as summer bedding plants. The plants are short-lived, but make good cut flowers.

CULTIVATION. Grow in well-drained, humus-rich soil in sun. Some support is useful from an early stage. Plant perennial species in spring or autumn. Propagate perennials by division at planting time, from seed or cuttings in spring.

RECOMMENDED. *C. auriculata*, *C. gigantea*, *C. grandiflora*, *C. lanceolata*, *C. rosea*, *C. verticillata*.

Coreopsis verticillata ▶

Cornus

A group of shrubs and perennials, plus a few trees, which are mainly hardy and deciduous. Some have brightly coloured bark, while others have attractive foliage, flowers or berries.

CULTIVATION. Grow in any humus-rich soil in sun or partial shade. Plant out autumn to spring. Propagate from seed when ripe, layering in spring, cuttings with a heel in late summer, suckers or and division of herbaceous types.

RECOMMENDED. *C. alba, C. florida, C. kousa, C. mas, C. nuttalli, C. sanguinea, C stolonifera.*

◀ *Cornus alba*

Corokia

A group of 3 evergreen, wiry stemmed shrubs from New Zealand. The flowers are starry yellow with berry-like fruit.

CULTIVATION. Grow in well-drained soil in a sunny, sheltered site. Half-hardy specimens need protection from frosts. Can be grown in a frost-free greenhouse. Plant or pot in spring. Propagate from seed in spring, or cuttings with a heel in late summer.

RECOMMENDED. *C. buddleioides, C. cotoneaster, C. macrocarpa, C. x virgata.*

Corokia x virgata

Coronilla

A group of 20 eye-catching perennials and shrubs with pea-shaped flowers and slender pods in between each seed. Ideal for softening garden steps or low, stone walls.

CULTIVATION. Grow in well-drained soil in sun; half-hardy species should be planted against a sheltered wall. Propagate from seed in spring, cuttings of young shoots in perennials, cuttings with a heel in late summer or the shrubs.

RECOMMENDED. *C. emerus, C. minima, C. montana, C. valentina, C. varia.*

◀ *Coronilla emerus*

Cortaderia

A large pampas grass with a densely tufted or clump-forming habit, arching leaves and plume-like, tiny spikelets.

CULTIVATION. Grow in well-drained soil in a sunny site. Plant spring or early autumn. Propagate by division or from seed in spring. Old foliage should be removed each spring.

RECOMMENDED. C. *richardii*, C. *selloana*, C.s. Monstrosa, C.s. Pumila, C.s. Rendatleri, C.s. Sunningdale Silver.

◀ *Cortaderia selloana* Sunningdale Silver

Corydalis

A group of low growing perennials that are generally tufted, sometimes tuberous, with fern-like, delicate leaves. The tubular flowers emerge upside down.

CULTIVATION. Needs humus-rich soil, preferably in light shade. Plant autumn or spring. Propagate from seed when ripe or in spring. Large plants can be divided after flowering or in spring.

RECOMMENDED. C. *ambugua*, C. *bulbosa*, C. *chielanthifolia*, C. *diphylla*, C. *lutea*, C. *solida*.

Corydalis solida

Corylopsis

A group of 20 species of shrubs and trees. Slender-twigged, bushy with prominently veined leaves and catkin-like small, fragrant flowers.

CULTIVATION. Plant in humus-rich, preferably acid or neutral soil in partial shade or sun. Plant autumn to spring. Propagate from ripe seed, cuttings with a heel in late summer or by layers in spring.

RECOMMENDED. C. *glabrescens*, C. *gotoana*, C. *pauciflora*, C. *platypetala*, C, *sinensis*, C. *willmottiae*.

◀ *Corylopsis glabrescens*

Corylus

A group of 15 species of deciduous shrubs and trees. They have toothed leaves. The males have catkin-like, small, fragrant flowers, while the female plants have bud-like flowers with red stigmas. The fruit is a nut surrounded by bracts.

CULTIVATION. Grow in humus-rich soil in sun or light shade. Plant autumn and winter. Propagate from seed when ripe or by layers in spring; suckers may also be used.

RECOMMENDED. *C. avellana, C.a. pendula, C. cornuta, C. maxima, C.m.* Purpurea.

Corylus maxima Purpurea ▶

Cosmos

This is a group of 25 species of annuals and perennials. Mainly erect plants with dissected leaves in opposite pairs, they have broad, daisy-like flower-heads.

CULTIVATION. Grow in moist soil in a sunny site. Sow seed under glass in spring; harden off and plant out when all danger of frost has passed in early summer. Seed can also be sown *in situ* in late spring to early summer. Support is advisable in windy locations.

RECOMMENDED. *C. bipinnatus, C. sulphureus.*

◀ *Cosmos bipinnatus*

Cotinus

Deciduous, grey bushes with rounded leaves and terminal slender, flowers stalks, some bearing tiny, 5-petalled flowers, while others are fine-haired, often pink or red-tinted, creating a smoky effect.

CULTIVATION. Grow in well-drained soil in a sunny site; some species prefer light shade. Plant autumn to spring. Propagate by cuttings with a heel in late summer, or by layering in spring.

RECOMMENDED. *C. coggygria, C.c.* Flame, *C.c.* Notcutts, *C.c purpureus, C.c.* Royal Purple.

Cotinus coggygria purpureus ▶

Cotoneaster

A group of mainly deciduous shrubs and trees, very popular as there is one to suit every position. The plants are susceptible to fireblight, a bacterial disease that can rapidly kill some members of this species. Symptoms can include branches withering for no obvious reason in the summer months. If this happens, cut back hard to the base of the affected branch, burn cuttings, disinfect secateurs and paint the open wound with a pruning solution. This will cure most cases. If symptoms persist, then fireblight may well be the reason and the plant will have to be dug up and burnt. The flowers are small, white to pinkish, 5-petalled and either solitary or in clusters. Fruit and decorative foliage produces additional interest and winter colour.

CULTIVATION. Grow in any well-drained soil, preferably in sun or light shade. Plant autumn to spring. Propagate by cuttings with a heel in late summer or from seed when ripe. Seed may take a year to germinate, particularly if allowed to dry out.

RECOMMENDED. C. *dammeri*, C. *franchetti*, C. *frigidus*, C. *horizaontalis*, C. *lateus*, C. *microphyllus*, C. *salicifolia*, C. *salicifolius*, C. *splendens*, C. x *watereri*.

Cotoneaster x *watereri* Exburiensis ▼

▲　*Cotoneaster franchettii*

Cotoneaster conspicuus ▲

▲　*Cotoneaster x wateri Rothschildianus*

Cotoneaster s. rugosa ▲

Cotula

A genus of 75 species of mainly small annuals and perennial plants. Most are mat-forming hardy plants with button-like flower-heads.

CULTIVATION. Grow in any soil, preferably one that does not dry out easily, in sun or light shade. Plant hardy species autumn to spring, half-hardy species when all frosts have passed. Propagate from seed in spring or by division of the perennials in late summer or spring.

RECOMMENDED. C. atrata, C. barbata, C. coronopifolia, C. potentillina, C. pyrethrifolia.

◀　*Cotula atrata*

Crambe

A genus of 25 species of mainly robust perennials. *C. cortifolia* is grown as a large, ornamental species. The leaves are fleshy, deep green and can be up to 1m long; stems to 2m or more tall, bearing numerous, small, white scented flowers. The effect resembles that of gypsophila in summer.

CULTIVATION. Grow in humus-rich soil in sun. Plant autumn to spring. Propagate from seed, by division or root-cuttings in spring.

RECOMMENDED. *C. cordifolia*, *C. maritima*.

Crambe cordifolia ▶

Crataegus

A group of deciduous shrubs and small trees, the hawthorn has shiny leaves and 5-petalled, white or pink flowers. The haws are generally red or orange in colour adding colour in autumn.

CULTIVATION. Grow in any well-drained soil in sun or light shade. Plant autumn to winter. Grafting onto rootstock or layering is not always successful. Seed provides the easiest method, but is slow to germinate.

RECOMMENDED. *C. flava*, *C. intricata*, *C. laciniata*, *C. laevigata*, *C. monogyna*, *C. pedicillata*.

◀ *Crataegus laciniata*

▼ *Crataegus laevigata*

Crataegus prunifolia ▼

Crepis

A genus of 200 species of annuals, biennials and perennials. Tufted plants with oblong leaves and erect flowering stems, they bear multiple flower-heads that resemble dandelion flowers.

CULTIVATION. Grow in any well-drained soil in a sunny site. Plant autumn or spring. Propagate from seed or division in spring.

RECOMMENDED. *C. aurea*, *C. incana*, *C. pygmacea*, *C. rubra*.

 Crepis incana

Crinum

A genus of bulbous-rooted perennials from the tropics and subtropics. They have long-necked bulbs, broad, fleshy leaves and erect, leafless stems bearing funnel-shaped, lily-like blossoms.

CULTIVATION. Half-hardy species can be grown in well-drained, sunny sites with the base of the bulbs at least 30cm below the soil surface. Colder areas require a frost-free greenhouse. Plant or pot in spring. Propagate by division in spring.

RECOMMENDED. *C. asiaticum*, *C. bulbispermum*, *C. macowanii*, *C. moorei*, *C.* x *powellii*.

Crinum moorei ▶

Crocosmia

Cormous plants with flattened, sword-like leaves, and arching, branched spikes of funnel-shaped flowers in late summer.

CULTIVATION. Grow in well-drained, humus-rich soil, which does not dry out, in sun or light shade. Plant in spring. Propagate either by division, offsets or from seed in spring.

RECOMMENDED. *C. aurea*, *C.* x *crocosmiiflora*, *C. masonorum*, *C. pottsii*.

 Crocosmia x *crocosmiiflora* Citronella

Crocus

A genus of approximately 75 species of cormous-rooted perennials. They have grassy leaves with a white or silvery central stripe and chalice-shaped blooms that expand in the sun. Each flower has three stamens only and a long, stalk-like tube near the corm. Most of the autumn-flowering species bloom before the leaves, but the winter and spring types flower with the foliage. After flowering, the leaves elongate greatly and before they die away, the seed capsules emerge above ground to ripen.

CULTIVATION. Grow in any, well-drained soil in a site that receives the low autumn to spring sun, otherwise the flowers will not open properly. Plant autumn-flowering species in late summer, the remainder in autumn. Propagate from seed sown when ripe or as soon afterwards as possible, offsets when dormant. All crocuses, make excellent plants for the cold greenhouse and several species are best grown in this way in areas of wet summers or where the soil does not dry out. Plant in pans of a loam-based compost and keep just moist until the leaves show, then water regularly. When the leaves start to yellow, keep dry until repotting time.

RECOMMENDED. *C. ancyrensis*, *C.a.* Golden Bunch, *C. asturicus*, *C. banaticus*, *C. biflorus*, *C. cancellatus*, *C. candidus*, *C. chrysanthus*, *C. ochroleucus*, *C. pulchellus*, *C. sativus*, *C. speciosus*, *C. ternus*, *C. vernus*.

▼ *Crocus ancyrensis* Golden Bunch

Crocus chrysanthus Cream Beauty ▼

▲ *Crocus biflorus weldenii*   *Crocus sativus* ▶

▲ *Crocus laevigatus*

Crocus speciosus Oxonian ▲

▲ *Crocus stellaris*

Crocus Vanguard ▲

Curtonus

A genus of one species of cormous-rooted perennials with a clump-forming habit. The sword-shaped leaves are long, pleated fans. The flowers are orange-red, trumpet-shaped with 6 oblong lobes in late summer.

CULTIVATION. Grow in any well-drained soil in a sunny site. Plant autumn or spring. Propagate by division or from offsets at planting time.

RECOMMENDED. *C. paniculatus.*

Curtonus paniculatus ▶

Cyananthus

A genus of 30 species of herbaceous perennials. Most species have blue or purple-blue flowers. Mainly alpines, they have prostrate stems and upturned, tubular flowers. Suitable specimens for rock gardens or scree.

CULTIVATION. Grow in well drained, neutral to acid soil with leaf mould or peat added, in sun. Plant spring or autumn. Propagate from seed or by cuttings of young shoots in spring.

RECOMMENDED. *C. lobatus*, *C.l.* Albus, *C.l. insignis*, *C.l.* Sherriff's, *C. microphyllus*.

◀   *Cyananthus microphyllus*

Cyclamen

There are 20 species of perennial plants from Europe, the Mediterranean to Iran. These are excellent specimens for semi-shade. These perennial plants have star-like foliage, often edged with silver. The solitary, pendant flowers have petals that resemble shuttlecocks.

CULTIVATION. Grow hardy species in humus-rich soil, preferably in light shade. They may also be grown in a frost-free greenhouse. Plant or re-plant when dormant. Propagate from seed sown when ripe or in spring. Grow tender species in a greenhouse, shaded from sun in summer and well ventilated. Propagate from seed in early autumn or late winter. Pot up into a mixture of peat and leaf mould for best results. When leaves start to yellow in late spring, dry off plants and store in a cool, dry place. In late summer, remove the tuber (corm). Shake off old soil and repot, keeping just moist until growth starts, then water more freely. It is usual to set the tubers with the upper part above the soil surface and to avoid pouring water into the centre of the growing plant.

RECOMMENDED. *C. balearicum*, *C. cilicium*, *C. coum*, *C. hederifolium*, *C. libanoticum*, *C. mirabile*, *C. purpurascens*, *C. repandum*.

 *Cyclamen vernum*

Cyclamen hederifolium

Cyclamen atkinsii

Cyclamen graecum

Cyclamen repandum

Cypripedium

A genus of 50 species of terrestrial orchids. Commonly known as Lady's Slipper, most plants are hardy, fibrous-rooted and clump-forming. The leaves are hairy and the flowers are generally large and can be solitary.

CULTIVATION. Grow in partial or dappled shade in a sheltered site. Neutral to acid rooting medium is required. Plant in spring. Propagate by careful division in spring.

RECOMMENDED. *C. acaule, C. calceolus, C. cordigerum, C. macrathanum, C. montanum.*

Cypripedium cordigerum

Cystoperis

There are 18 species of these small ferns that come from the Arctic, temperate and subtropical regions, mainly from mountains in warmer areas. They are tufted with 2–4 leaves.

CULTIVATION. Grow in partial shade in well-drained, but moisture-retentive, humus-rich soil. Plant autumn or spring. Propagate by spores or division in spring.

RECOMMENDED. *C. alpina, C. bulbifera, C. dickieana, C. fragilis, C. regia.*

◀ *Cystoperis bulbifera*

Cytisus

A genus of 30 species of deciduous and evergreen shrubs and trees. The flowers are pea-shaped followed by flattened pods.

CULTIVATION. Grow in well-drained soil in sun. The tender species need greenhouse treatment and any potting compost is suitable. Pot or repot in spring. Propagate from seed in spring or cuttings with a heel in late summer. Plant the hardy types directly into the flowering site.

RECOMMENDED. *C. ardonii, C. decumbens, C. multiflorus, C. nigricans, C. x spachianus.*

Cytisus x *spachianus*

Dahlia

A genus of 27 species of tuberous-rooted perennials from Mexico and Guatemala with solitary, daisy-like flower-heads. All are half-hardy-to-tender perennials and can be grown outside in cool temperature climates when all danger of frost has passed.

CULTIVATION. Grow in a well-drained, humus-rich soil that never dries out, in a sunny, preferably sheltered, location. Propagate by cuttings, from seed or by careful division of the tubers, making sure that a portion of the old stem with one good bud remains. This is best done just before planting in early summer when the buds are clearly visible. All except the dwarf bedding dahlias will require staking and it is best to insert stakes before planting to avoid root damage. Stop all young plants when 4–5 pairs of leaves have formed to encourage shapely, bushy specimens. Apply a mulch of well-decayed manure or compost. Lift tubers once frost has blackened the leaves in autumn, cutting stems back to 15cm and remove all the soil. Dry off upside down for a few days and then store in trays of dried peat in a frost-free place.

RECOMMENDED. Dahlias are categorised by their form and type of flower. They are all originally derived from forms of *D. variabilis*. Group 1 Single-flowered blooms: 'Coltness Gem' various colours; 'Mignon' mixed colours; 'Redskin' yellow and orange. Group 2 Anemone-flowered: 'Comet' scarlet; 'Scarlet Comet' bright red. Group 3 Collerette: 'Can Can' light purple with cream collar; 'Libretto' dark velvety-red with white collar. Group 4 Peony-flowered – semi-double blooms. Groups 5–6 Decorative – double blooms and often very large: 'Lady Linda' yellow, 'Chorus Girl' pink, 'Edinburgh' white and purple. Group 7 Ball – fully double, ball-shaped blooms. Group 8 Pompom – superb for bouquets and longlasting; 'Moor Place'; 'Small World'; 'Pensford Marion'. Groups 9–10 Cactus fully double blooms divided into Giant, Large, Medium, Small, Miniature: 'Apple Blossom' lilac-pink with paler centre; 'Choral' white; 'Doris Day' bright red; 'Orefeo' wine-red. Group 11 Semi-cactus; 'Park Princess'. Group 12 mostly clones.

▼ *Dahlia Enfield* Salmon

Dahlia Ruwenzori ▼

Daphne

A genus of 70 species of hardy, evergreen and deciduous shrubs from Europe, North Africa, Asia and the Pacific. This is a winter-flowering shrub with tubular, richly scented flowers and berry-like fruit.

CULTIVATION. Grow in any well-drained soil that does not dry out, preferably enriched with leaf mould or peat, in sun or partial shade. Plant evergreen varieties in autumn when they are in flower and are actively growing. Deciduous species should be planted in spring when all danger of frost has passed. Propagate by cuttings with a heel in late summer or from seed when ripe. Both rooted cuttings and seedlings should be grown on in pots and planted out into the flowering position as they transplant badly from the open ground.

RECOMMENDED. *D. aplina*, *D. bholua*, *D. caucasia*, *D. collina*, *D. mezereum*, *D. petraea*, *D.p.* Grandiflora, *D. pontica*, *D. retusa*, *D. tangutica*.

▼ *Daphne petraea* Grandiflora   *Daphne mezereum alba* ▼

▲ *Daphne* x *burkwoodii*   *Daphne blagayana* ▲

▲ *Daphne cneorum Eximia*

Daphne retusa ▲

Davidia

There is only one species of this deciduous tree with a conical habit. The bark is a purplish-brown colour, vertically fissured and flakes off. Also called the 'handkerchief tree', as the pure, white pendant bracts resemble handkerchiefs.

CULTIVATION. Grow in humus-rich soil in sun or partial shade in a sheltered site. Plant autumn to spring. Propagate by layering in spring, cuttings with a heel in late summer or from seed sown when ripe.

RECOMMENDED. *D. involucrata*, *D.i. villmoriniana*.

◀ *Davidia involucrata*

Decaisnea

A genus of two deciduous shrubs. In summer, long, drooping, yellowy-green blossoms, appear. The flowers are followed by cylindrical pod-like, fleshy fruit with a metallic purple-blue, edible skin.

CULTIVATION. Grow in humus-rich soil in partial shade or sun, sheltered from strong, cold winds. Plant autumn to spring. Propagate from seed in a cold frame when ripe.

RECOMMENDED. *D. fargesii*, *D. insignis*.

Decaisnea fargesii 'in fruit' ▶

Delphinium

A group of 250 species of annuals and herbaceous perennials. They have erect stems and produce towering spikes of single or semi-double flowers, coloured white to blue or violet. A popular specimen for cut flowers.

CULTIVATION. Grow in fertile, moisture-retentive soil, enriched with compost or well-decayed manure. The site should be sunny and sheltered from strong winds. Plant autumn to spring. Propagate all by seed either as soon as ripe or the following spring, for they are short-lived. Hardy annuals can also be sown *in situ* in mid-autumn for earlier blooms the following year. Propagate perennials by division or cuttings in early spring. Take cuttings just as the young leaves start to expand, severing below ground level, close to the crown. Place in a cold frame protected from severe frosts. Taller species will require staking. This should be done in spring.

RECOMMENDED. *D. ambiguum, D. cardinale, D. chinensis, D. elatum, D. formosum, D. grandiflorum, D. menziesii, D. muscosum, D. nudicaule.*

▼ *Delphinium nudicaule*

▲ *Delphinium* typical garden hybrids

Delphinium typical garden hybrids ▲

▲ *Delphinium* University Hybrid

Delphinium garden *hybrids* ▲

Dendromecon

Evergreen shrubs from with a stiff, erect habit and alternate, leathery leaves. The fragrant flowers are bright yellow, cup-shaped and open almost flat summer to autumn.

CULTIVATION. Grow in well-drained soil, against a sunny, sheltered wall in all but the mildest areas. Liable to suffer winter frost damage if no protection is given. Plant or pot in spring. Propagate from seed sown in spring or cuttings taken in late summer or early autumn.

RECOMMENDED. *D. rigida.*

◀   *Dendromecon rigida*

Dentaria

A group of 20 herbaceous perennials with underground rhizomes and four-petalled flowers

CULTIVATION. Grow in humus-rich soil that does not dry out, in partial or dappled shade. Plant after flowering or autumn to spring. Propagate by division at planting time or from seed in spring.

RECOMMENDED. *D. enneaphylla, D. heptaphylla, D. pentaphylla.*

Dentaria pentaphylla ▶

Deutzia

A genus of 50 deciduous shrubs. allied to the Philadelphus, with opposite pairs of leaves and starry, 5-petalled flowers.

CULTIVATION. Grow in any fertile, well-drained soil in sun or light shade. They are prone to late spring frosts and should have a sheltered site against a wall and in a sunny position. Propagate by softwood cuttings in summer or hardwood cuttings in autumn, grown on in a cold frame.

RECOMMENDED. *D. corymbosa, D. discolour, D. gracilis, D. longifolia, D. pulchra, D. purpurascens.*

◀   *Deutzia corymbosa*

Dianthus

A large group of 300 species of annuals and perennials with evergreen, blue-green leaves. Easy to grow, the flowers have strong scent and are brightly coloured.

CULTIVATION. Grow in any well-drained soil in a sunny site, preferably on rock gardens, dry walls, raised or scree beds. Plant autumn to spring. Propagate by cuttings in summer or from seed in spring to summer, in a cold frame.

RECOMMENDED. *D. alpinus, D. caryophyllus, D. chinensis, D. neglectus, D. pulmarius, D. superbus.*

Dianthus alpinus ▶

Diascia

A genus of 45 species of annuals and perennials from S. Africa. They vary in habit from erect to prostrate, with oval leaves and erect, 5-petalled flowers.

CULTIVATION. Grow in well-drained, humus-rich soil in a sheltered, sunny site. In colder areas, provide protection in a cold frame. Propagate annuals from seed sown under glass and the perennials by cuttings in spring or from seed in spring.

RECOMMENDED. *D. barbarae, D. cordata.*

◀ *Diascia cordata*

Dicentra

Herbaceous perennials that are clump-forming in habit. The leaves are fern-like and the flowers are 4-petalled pendants.

CULTIVATION. Grow in humus-rich soil in sun or shade. Plant autumn to spring. Propagate by division at planting time or root cuttings in late winter in a cold frame.

RECOMMENDED. *D. cucullaria, D. eximia, D. formosa, D. spectabilis.*

Dicentra spectabilis ▶

Digitalis

A genus of 26 species of biennials, perennials and shrubs, the foxglove is ideally suited to gardens with a moist, slightly acid soil. The leaves are hairy and there are dense spikes of thimble-shaped, purplish-pink flowers.

CULTIVATION. Grow in humus-rich soil in sun or shade. Propagate from seed in late spring and plant in permanent site in autumn or spring.

RECOMMENDED. *D. feruginea, D. dubia, D. grandiflora, D. lutea, D. purpurea.*

Digitalis grandiflora ▶

Dimorphotheca

Also known as Osteospermum, these dwarf daisies are true sun lovers. They open their flowers as soon as the sun appears and close them at the first sign of clouds. Not generally hardy, so bring undercover in winter.

CULTIVATION. Grow in a well-drained soil in a sunny, sheltered site. Propagate from seed in spring or take cuttings in late summer and overwinter young plants.

RECOMMENDED. *D. aurantiaca, D. barbariae, D. calendulacea, D. ecklonis.*

◀ *Dimorphotheca aurantiaca* cultivars

Dipelta

A group of 4 species of deciduous shrubs from China with scented, foxglove-like flowers and small, seed capsules attached to rounded bracts. An easy plant to grow.

CULTIVATION. Grow in any well-drained soil, preferably humus-enriched, in sun or partial shade. Plant autumn to spring. Propagate by cuttings with a heel in late summer. Cut back after flowering to ground level.

RECOMMENDED. *D. floribunda, D. yunnanensis.*

Dipelta floribunda ▶

Dodecatheon

These are tufted herbaceous, perennials with slender, leafless, flowering stems that produce nodding, cyclamen-like flowers.

CULTIVATION. Grow in moisture-retentive, humus-rich soil in sun or partial shade. Plant after flowering or autumn to spring. Propagate from seed or by division. Some species produce rice grain-like bulblets at the root bases, which can be carefully detached and treated as seed.

RECOMMENDED. *D. alpinum*, *D. clevelandii*, *D. dentatum*, *D. jeffreyi*, *D. meadia*, *D. pulchellum*.

◀ *Dodecatheon meadia*

Doronicum

A genus of 35 herbaceous, clump-forming perennials with erect stems and unusually narrow-stemmed leaves. The daisy-like flowers are bright yellow in colour.

CULTIVATION. Grow in any well-drained, but moisture-retentive soil in sun or light shade. Plant autumn to spring. Propagate by division at planting time or from seed in spring.

RECOMMENDED. *D. austriacum*, *D. columnae*, *D. cordatum*, *D. pardalianches*, *D. plantagineum*, *D.p.* Harpur Crewe.

Doronicum plantagineum ▶

Dorotheanthus

Also know as Livingstone Daisy, this annual plant is prostrate, mat-forming with almost cylindrical leaves. The daisy-like flowers appear in shades of red, pink, white or bicoloured with dark centres in summer.

CULTIVATION. Grow in well-drained soil in a sunny site. Sow seed thinly *in situ* in late spring, or for a longer display, early to mid-spring under glass.

RECOMMENDED. *D. bellidiformis*.

 Dorotheanthus bellidiformis

Draba

A genus of 300 species of annuals and perennials. Most are cushion-forming and bear 4-petalled, mainly yellow, flowers in spring.

CULTIVATION. Grow in sharply-drained, gritty soil in sun, ideally on rock gardens. Some species require protection from winter wet and are best planted in an alpine house. Plant autumn or spring. Propagate from seed in spring, cuttings in late summer or careful division where possible.

RECOMMENDED. *D. azoides, D. borealis, D. bruniifolia, D. dedeana.*

◀ *Draba azoides*

Dryas

A genus of two evergreen species of prostrate shrubs with oblong leaves and solitary, 8–10-petalled flowers.

CULTIVATION. Grow in well-drained, preferably limy and gritty soil in a sunny site. Plant autumn to spring. Propagate from seed when ripe, cuttings with a heel in late summer or by layering in spring.

RECOMMENDED. *D. drummondii, D. octopetala, D.o. lanata, D.o. minor, D.o. tenella.*

Dryas octopetala

Dryopteris

A genus of 150 species of evergreen and deciduous ferns that prefer damp areas of the garden. They have thick, short rhizomes of generally bi- or tripinnate fronds.

CULTIVATION. Grow in humus-rich soil in shade or sun, preferably sheltered from strong winds. Plant autumn to spring. Propagate plants with 2 or more crowns by division at planting time or by spores in spring.

RECOMMENDED. *D. cristata, D. dilatata, D. erythrosora, D. filix-mas, D. pseudo-mas.*

◀ *Dryopteris pseudo-mas*

Echinacea

One of the most familiar, herbaceous perennials in older gardens. Clump-forming, with edible roots, erect, leafy stems and large, daisy-like flower-heads.

CULTIVATION. Grow in humus-rich, well-drained, but moisture-retentive, soil in a sunny site. Plant in early spring. Propagate by division at planting time or from seed in spring.

RECOMMENDED. *E. angustifolia, E. pallida, E. purpurea.*

Echinacea purpurea Robert Bloom ▶

Echium

A genus of 40 species of annuals, perennials and shrubs. The leaves are covered in coarse hairs and the flowers are funnel-shaped, clustered together.

CULTIVATION. Grow in a frost-free, airy, sunny greenhouse for half-hardy types; a sunny border for hardy types. Both need well-drained soil. Propagate hardy biennials *in situ* from seed in late summer or grow as annuals. Propagate half-hardy species from seed in late spring.

RECOMMENDED. *E. callithyrsum, E. fastuosum, E. lycopsis, E. pininiana, E. wildpretii.*

◀ *Echium lycopsis* Dwarf Bedding Mixed

Edraianthus

A genus of 10 species of small, perennial plants. Tufted in habit with grassy leaves, the small, stalkless bellflowers appear in summer.

CULTIVATION. Grow in sharply-drained soil in a sunny site. Plant autumn or spring. Propagate from seed sown in spring or cuttings of basal shoots, inserted into coarse sand, in a cold frame in spring.

RECOMMENDED. *E. dalmaticus, E. dinaricus, E. graminifolius, E. pumilio, E. serpyllifolius.*

Edraianthus serpyllifolius ▶

Elaeagnus

A group of 45 species of evergreen and deciduous shrubs. They often have spiny stems and small, tubular or bell-shaped flowers. The fleshy berries are edible.

CULTIVATION. Grow in well-drained, preferably in sun, but evergreen species will stand partial shade. All species grow well near the sea. Plant autumn to spring. Propagate by cuttings with a heel in summer or from seed when ripe.

RECOMMENDED. *E. angustifolia*, *E. commutata*, *E. glabra*, *E. multiflora*, *E. pungens*, *E. umbellata*.

Elaeagnus pungens Maculata ▷

Elsholtzia

A genus of 35 species of sub-shrubs and perennials. *E. stauntonii* is the most widely available. This is a deciduous plant, the current season's growth of which dies back in winter. The leaves smell strongly of mint when bruised. The tubular flowers are a lilac-purple colour.

CULTIVATION. Grow in well-drained, humus-rich soil. Plant autumn to spring. Propagate by cuttings in summer.

RECOMMENDED. *E. stauntonii*.

◁ *Elsholtzia stauntonii*

Elymus

A genus of 70 species of perennial grasses. A robust, rhizomatous grass, forming extensive colonies. Leaves are bright blue-grey with flowering spikelets in pairs in summer. A good foliage plant, but apt to be invasive.

CULTIVATION. Grow in any well-drained soil in sun. Plant spring or autumn. Propagate by division at planting time.

RECOMMENDED. *E. arenarius*.

Elymus arenarius ▷

Epilobium

A group of 200 species of perennials and sub-shrubs. They have prostrate to erect stems and 4-petalled flowers that can be solitary.

CULTIVATION. Grow in sun in any well-drained, moisture-retentive soil. Plant out autumn to spring. Propagate by division, or from seed sown in shade outdoors, or a cold frame. New Zealand species may not be fully hardy.

RECOMMENDED. *E. chloraefolium*, *E. crassum*, *E. doonaei*, *E. glabellum*, *E. obcordatum*.

 Epilobium glabellum

Epimedium

A group of 21 species of evergreen and deciduous perennials. Clump and colony forming, they have long stalks that can be flushed with colour in spring.

CULTIVATION. Grow in humus-rich soil in partial shade or sun. Plant after flowering or autumn to spring. Propagate by division at planting time or from ripe seed; seed can take 18 months to germinate.

RECOMMENDED. *E. alpinum*, *E. grandiflorum*, *E. macranthum*, *E. pinnatum*, *E. pubigerum*.

Epimedium x *youngianum* Niveum

Eranthis

A group of 7 species of perennials. Both leaves and flowering stems grow directly from tuber-like rhizomes. The leaves are umbrella-like. Flowers are buttercup-like blooms of 5–8 petals.

CULTIVATION. Grow in humus-rich soil in sun or shade. Plant in early autumn or soon afterwards. Propagate by separating offsets when dormant or division of clumps at flowering time.

RECOMMENDED. *E. cilicus*, *E. hyemalis*, *E. x tubergenii*.

 Eranthis cilicus

Erica

A genus of 600 species of evergreen shrubs or small trees. They are wiry stemmed with oblong leaves and small, bell to urn-shaped flowers often carried in profusion. The plants live in association with a fungus that permeates the whole plant. This fungus needs acid conditions, therefore nearly all *Erica* species need acid-peaty soil to thrive.

CULTIVATION. Grow the hardy species in a sunny site, the tender species under glass with good ventilation. Plant hardy species in autumn or spring, using one third acid, all peat composts. Propagate by cuttings with a heel in late summer for hardy types, or spring for tender ones. Hardy *Ericas* benefit from shearing over after flowering and greenhouse types should have all spent flower-spikes and a few centimetres of stem below removed when flowers fade.

RECOMMENDED. *E. arborea, E. australis, E. ciliaris, E. cinerea, E. x darlyeensis, E. x Darly Dale, E. erigena, E. gracillis, E. herbacea, E. lusitanica, E. pageana, E. scoparia, E. terminalis, E. tetralix, E. umbellata, E. vagans, E. x watsonii.*

▼   *Erica herbacea* cultivars

▲ *Erica* x *watsonii* Dawn

▲ *Erica vagans* Mrs Maxwell

Erica cinerea ▼

▲ *Erica cinerea* Cevennes

Erica tetralix Alba Mollis ▼

Erigeron

A genus of 200 species of annuals and perennials. They are mainly erect, clump-forming with daisy-like flower-heads, which resemble those of the *Aster*.

CULTIVATION. Grow in well-drained, fertile soil in a sunny site. Plant autumn to spring. Propagate by division at planting time or from seed in spring.

RECOMMENDED. *E. alpinus, E. aurantiacus, E. aureus, E. compositus, E. leiomerus, E. mucronatus, E. simplex, E. trifidus.*

Erigeron Foerster's Leibling ▶

Erinacea

A genus of one species of dwarf shrub commonly known as hedgehog broom, or blue broom. A hummock-forming shrub with silver-haired leaves. The flowers are pea-shaped and a blue-violet colour.

CULTIVATION. Grow in any well-drained soil in mild areas. Plant autumn or spring. Propagate from seed in spring in a cold frame.

RECOMMENDED. *E. anthyllis.*

 Erinacea anthyllis

Erodium

A genus of 90 species of annuals and perennials,that are allied to the geranium and pelargonium, having 5-petalled flowers.

CULTIVATION. Grow in any well-drained soil in a sunny site. Plant autumn or spring. Propagate by division, cuttings of roots or basal shoots or from seed in spring.

RECOMMENDED. *E. chrysanthum, E. corsicum, E. daucoides, E. guttatum, E. manescavii, E. pelargoniiflorum, E. petraeum, E. reichardii.*

Erodium reichardii ▶

Eryngium

A genus of 230 species of mainly herbaceous and evergreen perennials. They are tuft-forming with heart-shaped leaves. The tiny flowers are coloured purple, blue, whitish or greenish.

CULTIVATION. Grow in well-drained soil in a sunny site. Plant early autumn or spring. Propagate from seed or by careful division in spring or root cuttings in late winter.

RECOMMENDED. *E. agavifolium*, *E. alpinum*, *E. bourgatii*, *E. bromeliifolium*, *E. giganteum*, *E. maritimum*, *E. planum*.

◀ *Eryngium proteiflorum*

Erysimum

A genus of 100 species of annuals, biennials and perennials. A good, dry garden specimen.

CULTIVATION. Grow in warm site, at the base of a south-facing wall, in well-drained, humus-rich soil. May also be grown in pots in a greenhouse. Propagate from seed or soft cuttings with a heel in spring.

RECOMMENDED. *E. linifolium*.

Erysimum linifolium ▶

Erythrina

A genus of 100 species mainly of trees and shrubs with pea-shaped flowers followed by knobbly pods. Leaves can be leathery with prickly stalks. The flowers are scarlet coloured in summer.

CULTIVATION. Grow in a warm site, at the base of a south facing wall, in well-drained, humus-rich soil. Protect the crown from late autumn to spring. May also be grown in pots in a frost-free greenhouse. Pot or plant in spring. Propagate from seed or by soft cuttings with a heel in spring.

RECOMMENDED. *E. crista-galli*.

◀ *Erythrina crista-galli*

Erythronium

A group of 25 species of herbaceous perennials. The leaves are glossy and sometimes mottled. Flowers are pale coloured and solitary, opening in spring.

CULTIVATION. Grow in humus-rich soil, in shade. Plant early autumn. Propagate from seed and remove offsets when dormant.

RECOMMENDED. E. albidum, E. americanum, E. californicum, E. grandiflorum, E. hendersonii, E. howellii, E. oregonum.

Erythronium Pagoda

 *Erythronium dens-canis*

Erythronium oregonum White Beauty ▼

Escallonia

A group of 60 species of shrubs and small trees. They are mainly evergreen with fine-toothed leaves. The flowers are 5-petalled, tubular based. Most are tender.

CULTIVATION. Grow in well-drained soil in a sunny site, the less hardy types against a wall; all do well near the sea. Plant in spring. Propagate by cuttings with a heel in late summer or from seed.

RECOMMENDED. E. bifida, E. floribunda, E. rubra, E. virgata.

Escallonia x *iveyi* ▶

Eucalyptus

A genus of up to 600 species of fast-growing, evergreen trees and shrubs. The foliage is aromatic, but the shrubs are sensitive to cold so protect them from cold winds.

CULTIVATION. Grow in well-drained soil in a sunny site. Plant out in summer. Protect young plants from frost. Propagate from seed.

RECOMMENDED. *E. citriodora, E. coccifera, E. cordifolia, E. glutinosa, E. gunnii, E. x intermedia, E. lucida, E. milligarnii, E. nicholii, E. pauciflora, E. penniniana, E. pulverulenta, E. urnigera.*

◀ *Eucalyptus gunnii* juvenile

Eucomis

A genus of 14 species of bulbous perennials that have enlarged bulbs, fleshy leaves and star-shaped flowers in shades of green or white.

CULTIVATION. Grow in well-drained soil in warm areas or in a sheltered site. Plant spring or autumn. Good pot plants. Propagate by offsets or from seed.

RECOMMENDED. *E. comosa, E. cordifolia, E. glutinosa, E. lucida, E. moorei, E. poleevansii.*

Eucomis comosa ▶

Eucryphia

A group of 5 species of evergreen and deciduous trees and shrubs. They have 4-petalled, white flowers from late summer to autumn.

CULTIVATION. Provide a sheltered site in sun or light shade with neutral to acid soil that retains moisture. Plant in spring, hardier types in autumn. Propagate by layering in spring, cuttings with a heel in late summer.

RECOMMENDED. *E. cordifolia, E. glutinosa, E. lucida, E. moorei.*

◀ *Eucryphia glutinosa*

Euonymus

A genus of 176 species of deciduous or evergreen, spreading trees or shrubs. The small flowers are insignificant, but the seed is comparatively large.

CULTIVATION. Grow in any well-drained soil in sun or partial shade. Plant autumn to spring. Pruning is generally unnecessary, but the evergreen species can be clipped into shape. *E. japonicus* makes a good hedge, especially near the sea. Propagate from seed when ripe, by cuttings with a heel in late spring or late summer or by layering in spring.

RECOMMENDED. *E. alatus, E. europaeus, E. fortunei, E. hamiltonianus, E. japonicus, E. latifolius, E. oxyphyllus, E. phellomanus, E. planipes, E. sachalinensis.*

 Euonymus alatus in autumn

Euphorbia

A genus of 2,000 species of annuals, perennials, shrubs and succulents that vary greatly in form.

CULTIVATION. Grow the hardy and half-hardy species in any well-drained soil in a sunny site. Plant autumn to spring. Sow hardy annuals *in situ* in spring, half-hardy species under glass. Propagate from seed, by division or by cuttings of basal shoots.

RECOMMENDED. *E. capitulata, E. characias, E. griffithii, E. lathyris, E. mellifera, E. rigida.*

◀   *Euphorbia characias wulfenii*

Euryops

A genus of 70 species of evergreen shrubs. Fairly hardy with silvery-grey, hairy leaves. The flowers are solitary, daisy-like, canary-yellow and appear in late spring to summer.

CULTIVATION. Grow in well-drained soil in a mild, sunny site, autumn to spring. Can be planted in large tubs. Propagate by cuttings in spring.

RECOMMENDED. *E. acraeus.*

Euryops acraeus

Exacum

A genus of 40 species of annuals, biennials and perennials. One species is generally available; *E. affine*. This is a bushy annual with shiny leaves and 5-petalled, bluish-purple flowers with a central cone of yellow stamens.

CULTIVATION. A greenhouse specimen with light shade and good ventilation in summer. Sow seed in spring or in autumn for larger, earlier-flowering specimens the following year.

RECOMMENDED. *E. affine.*

◀   *Exacum affine*

Fatsia

A genus of 2 species of evergreen shrubs, but only one is commonly grown: *Fatsia japonica*. The leaves are glossy and leathery and the flowers are a milky-white colour, followed by glossy, black berries in late autumn.

CULTIVATION. Grow in mild areas in well-drained, humus-rich soil in sun or shade. Can be grown in pots or as a tub specimen. Plant autumn or spring. Propagate from seed in spring or cuttings in late summer.

RECOMMENDED. *F. japonica.*

Fatsia japonica

Feijoa

A genus of 2 species of evergreen shrubs. *F. sellowiana* is generally available. The leaves are dark green with a whitish underside. Flowers are red in the centre, fading to almost white at the margins.

CULTIVATION. Not fully hardy so protection is needed, either against a south wall or in a green-house. Propagate from cuttings taken with a heel in summer.

RECOMMENDED. *F. sellowiana*

Feijoa sellowiana

Felicia

A genus of 60 species of mainly dwarf-like sub-shrubs and annuals. The plant's flowers have daisy-like heads.

CULTIVATION. Grow half-hardy species in well-drained soil in sunny site. Plant in spring after frosts have passed. Provide protection in winter. Propagate perennials by cuttings in summer, annuals from seed in spring.

RECOMMENDED. *F. amelloides, F. bergeriana, F. pappei.*

Felicia bergeriana

Festuca

A genus of 80 species of perennial, tufted grasses. The leaves are long, narrow, evergreen and a blue colour. It forms dense, round clumps and is an ideal border plant.

CULTIVATION. Plant in any well-drained soil in a sunny site. Plant ornamentals in autumn to spring. Propagate from seed or by division autumn or spring.

RECOMMENDED. *F. galcialis, F. glauca, F. ovina, F. punctoria, F. rubra, F.r. commutata.*

 Festuca glauca

Filipendula

A genus of 10 species of herbaceous perennials with erect stems bearing large, terminal clusters of tiny, 5-petalled flowers with prominent stamens.

CULTIVATION. Grow in any moisture-retentive soil. *F. vulgaris* thrives best in a bog or waterside location. Plant autumn to spring. Propagate by division at planting time or from seed in spring.

RECOMMENDED. *F. kamtschatica, F. palmata, F. purpurea, F. rubra, F. ulmaria, F. vulgaris.*

Filipendula vulgaris Plena

 Filipendula palmata

 *Filipendula ulmaria* Aurea

Forsythia

A genus of 6 or 7 species of deciduous shrubs from South East Europe to Asia. They have simple or 3-cleft leaves and yellow, bell-like flowers before the leaves unfurl.

CULTIVATION. Grow in any well-drained garden soil in sun, although some shade is tolerated. Plant autumn to spring. Propagate by tip cuttings in summer or hard wood cuttings in autumn. Seed may be sown when ripe or in spring.

RECOMMENDED. *F. giraldiana, F. x intermedia, F. ovata, F. suspensa, F.s. atrocaulus, F.s. sieboldii.*

Forsythia suspensa atrocaulus ▶

Fothergilla

A genus of 2 species of deciduous shrubs with coarsely toothed leaves. The small, petalless flowers, appear in terminal bottle-brush spikes with long, white stamens.

CULTIVATION. Grow in moist but well-drained, like-free, peaty soil in sun or light shade. Plant autumn to spring. Propagate from ripe seed, layering or suckers in spring or cuttings with a heel in late summer.

RECOMMENDED. *F. agardenii, F. major, F. monticola.*

◀ *Fothergilla major* in autumn

Fragaria

A genus of 15 species of evergreen perennials with tufted runners and 5-petalled flowers followed by conical fruit.

CULTIVATION. Grow in any well-drained, fertile soil in sun or light shade. Plant autumn to spring. Propagate from seed when ripe or in spring, or by detached runners.

RECOMMENDED. *F. x anassa, F. x Variegata, F. californica, F. chiloensis, F. indica, F. vesca, F.v. monophylla, F. virginiana.*

Fragaria vesca ▶

Fuschia

A genus of about 100 species of shrubs and small trees. The flowers are composed of a tube with 4 petals forming a bell, sometimes with contrasting colours. The fruits are oblong or rounded and accompanied by purplish berries. The species and hybrid cultivars are mostly half-hardy and grown as greenhouse or house pot plants, with good ventilation and light shading in summer. In milder areas, most of these plants can be grown outside with winter protection and several are hardy in all but the severest of winters.

CULTIVATION. Any well-drained, fertile soil is suitable, preferably in sun, although light shade is tolerated. Plant outside when fear of frost has passed. In cold areas, apply a winter mound of weathered ashes, coarse sand or peat around the base of each plant. In spring, clear this away and cut back to remove all dead and frosted stems. In very cold areas, lift the plants in late autumn, pot or box and place in a frost-free frame or greenhouse. Staking will be required for standard species. Hanging basket cultivars need pinching out to build up a strong plant, bush plants will also require this to form well-branched specimens.

RECOMMENDED. *F. austromontana, F. corymbiflora, F. excorticata, F. fulgens, F. x hybrida, F. magellanica, F.m. gracilis, F.m.g. Variegata, F.m.g. Tricolour, F.m. molinae, F.m. Pumila, F. microphylla, F. procumbens, F. thymifolia, F. triphylla.*

▼ *Fuschia* cascade

Fuschia fulgens ▼

▼ *Fuschia* Southgate

Fuschia Mission Bells ▼

Galanthus

A genus of about 20 species of bulbous perennials. Each bulb has 2 narrow leaves, sometimes 3. They may be rolled together or pressed flat together. The solitary, white flowers have green tips and form a cup.

CULTIVATION. Grow in any well-drained, but moisture-retentive, soil, preferably humus-rich. Adequate water is necessary winter to spring for the plants to establish themselves.

RECOMMENDED. G. caucasicus, G. elwesii, G.e. maxima, G. ikariae, G. nivalis, G. plicatus.

Galanthus ikariae

Galium

A genus of 400 species of annuals and perennials. One species is generally available; G. odoratum. This plant forms large patches with white, tubular, fragrant flowers in early summer.

CULTIVATION. Grow in any well-drained, moisture-retentive soil in sun or shade. Plant autumn to spring. Propagate by division at planting time.

RECOMMENDED. G. odoratum.

◀ *Galium odoratum*

Garrya

A genus of 15 species of evergreen trees and shrubs. One hardy species is readily available; G. elliptica, commonly known as silk tassel bush. A vigorous shrub or small tree with lustrous, wavy-margined leaves, grey-woolly beneath. The flowers are in pendant catkins and appear in late winter.

CULTIVATION. Grow in any well-drained soil, in full sun. Best on a south wall in colder areas. Plant autumn or spring.

RECOMMENDED. G. elliptica.

Garrya elliptica

Gazania

A genus of 40 species of evergreen perennials. Prostrate or semi-prostrate with leaves that are dark green above and grey-white felted beneath. The daisy-like flowers are orange, red or yellow.

CULTIVATION. Grow in any well-drained soil in a sunny, sheltered site. Generally grown as half-hardy, they can survive in warm borders. Sow seed in spring and plant out when frost has passed. Cuttings can be taken in late summer.

RECOMMENDED. G. *bracteata*, G. *pavonia*, G. *pinnata*, G. *ringens*, G. *uniflora*, G. x *splendens*.

◀ *Gazania hybrids*

Genista

A genus of 75 species of deciduous shrubs and small trees, commonly known as broom. Their bright yellow flowers appear in spring through to summer and the gentle shade they create, allows for underplanting.

CULTIVATION. Grow in well-drained soil in a sunny site. Tender species will need greenhouse treatment. Propagate from seed in spring or cuttings with a heel in late summer.

RECOMMENDED. G. *cinerea*, G. *fragrans*, G. *hispanica*, G. *lydia*, G. *pilosa*, G. *tinctoria*.

Genista cinerea ▶

Gentiana

A genus of 350 species of annuals and perennials with tufted leaves and beautiful funnel or bell-shaped flowers. They can be mat-forming or tall stemmed.

CULTIVATION. Grow in well-drained, but moisture-retentive, humus-rich soil; acid is needed for some species. Plant in spring. Propagate by careful division at planting time, basal cuttings in spring or from seed when ripe.

RECOMMENDED. G. *asclepiadea*, G. *clusii*, G. *farreri*, G. *lutea*, G. *purdomii*, G. *verna*.

◀ *Gentiana verna*

Geranium

A genus of 400 species, mainly annuals and perennials. They are tufted, clump-forming, with long-stalked, rounded leaves. The 5-petalled flowers may be bowl or saucer-shaped, flattened or turned backwards. They are followed by long-beaked fruit that splits suddenly when ripe, scattering out the seeds. They quickly form large clumps of flowers, usually in shades of pink, mauve or blue. For the familiar pot and bedding geraniums see *Pelargonium*.

CULTIVATION. Grow in any well-drained garden soil, preferably in a sunny site, although some species can withstand partial shade. Plant autumn to spring. Propagate by division at planting time or from seed sown in spring.

RECOMMENDED. G. *cinereum*, G. *dalmaticum*, G.*d*. Album, G. *endressii*, G. *farreri*, G. *grandiflorum*, G. *himalayense*, G. *macrorrhizum*, G. *nodosum*, G. *phaeum*, G. *platypetalum*, G. *pratense*, G.*p*. Johnson's Blue, G. *pilostemon*, G. *pylzowianum*, G. *reflexum*, G. *renardii*, G. *sanguineum*, G.*s*. lancastrense, G. *sessiliflorum*, G.*s*. nigricans, G. *stapfianum*, G. *subcaulescens*, G. *sylvaticum*, G. *traversii*, G. *tuberosum*, G. *wallichianum*. G.*w*. Buxton's Blue, G. *wlassovianum*.

▼ *Geranium dalmaticum*

Geranium cinereum Ballerina ▼

▼ *Geranium himalayense*

Geranium renardii ▼

Geum

A genus of 40 species of herbaceous and ever-green perennials. They are tufted to clump-forming, with 5-petalled flowers, nodding and bell-like with a wide-opening habit.

CULTIVATION. Grow in any well-drained, but moisture-retentive soil in sun or light shade. Plant autumn to spring. Propagate by division at planting time, from seed when ripe or in spring.

RECOMMENDED. G. x *borisii*, G. *chiloense*, G. *montanum*, G. *reptans*, G. *rivale*, G. *urbanum*.

 Geum montanum

Gilia

A genus of annuals, biennials and perennials of approximately 120 species. One hardy annual is widely available; G. *capitata*. The flowers are tubular with lavender-blue, rounded heads, appearing in summer to autumn.

CULTIVATION. Grow in well-drained, preferably humus-rich soil, in a sunny site. Sow seed *in situ*, early autumn or spring. Support will be needed in exposed areas.

RECOMMENDED. G. *capitata*.

Gilia capitata

Gillenia

A genus of two species of herbaceous perennials, one of which is generally available; G. *trifoliata*. A clump-forming species with reddish stems and toothed leaves. The flowers are white, 5-petalled, starry and appear in summer.

CULTIVATION. Grow in humus-rich, moist soil preferably in partial shade. Plant autumn to spring. Propagate by division at planting time or from seed in spring. An easy to raise plant.

RECOMMENDED. G. *trifoliata*.

 Gillenia trifoliata

Gladiolus

A genus of 200 species cormous-rooted plants that produce broadly sword-shaped leaves in fan-like tufts and widely funnel-shaped flowers. Each bloom has a short, curving tube and six petals. Most colours are available except true blue. Best planted in groups to create huge swathes of colour.

CULTIVATION. Grow in well-drained, humus-rich soil in sun. Plant half-hardy corms in late spring. Hardy species may be planted in autumn. Tender species are grown under glass. Staking is needed or tying to twine.

RECOMMENDED. G. *carneus*, G. x *colvillei*, G. *imbricatus*, G. Oscar, G. *papilio*, G. *tristis*.

▼ *Gladiolus byzantinus*

Gladiolus Columbine ▼

Gladiolus Oscar ▼

▼ *Gladiolus* Melodie

Griselinia

A genus of 6 species of evergreen shrubs and trees with tiny, 5-petalled, greenish flowers, followed by fleshy, berry-like fruit.

CULTIVATION. Grow in well-drained, humus-rich soil in sun or light shade, preferably in mild areas or by the sea. Propagate by cuttings with a heel in late summer or from seed in spring.

RECOMMENDED. G. *littoralis*, G.l. *variegata*, G. *lucida*.

 Griselinia littoralis

Gunnera

A genus of 50 species of evergreen and deciduous perennials. Clump-forming with tufted leaves. The greenish flower spikes are very small with only two petals. They are followed by berry-like fruit.

CULTIVATION. Grow in moist to wet, humus-rich soil in sun or light shade. Plant in spring. Propagate from seed when ripe or by division at planting time.

RECOMMENDED. G. *magellanica*, G. *manicata*, G. *tinctoria*.

Gunnera manicata

Gypsophila

A genus of 125 species of perennials and annuals with either an erect, prostrate or cushion-forming habit. The clusters of flowers are 5-petalled, white to rose-pink in colour.

CULTIVATION. Grow in sunny sites in well-drained soil. Plant perennials autumn to spring. Sow seed of annuals *in situ* in spring or autumn in sheltered areas. Propagate perennials from seed, root or stem cuttings in spring.

RECOMMENDED. G. *cerastoides*, G. *elegans*, G.e. Paris Market, G. *paniculata*, G. *repens*.

 Gypsophila repens

Hacquetia

A small, clump-forming, herbaceous perennial with bright green leaves. The 5-petalled flowers are tiny, set in greenish-yellow axils.

CULTIVATION. Grow in a moist, cool situation and in partial shade, preferably in heavy loam or clay soil or enriched with humus.

RECOMMENDED. *H. epipactis.*

Hacquetia epipactis

Hakonechloa

A perennial grass, formerly classified as a reed, which forms colonies. The stems can be erect or spreading, with linear, pointed leaves, greenish or yellowish depending on variety.

CULTIVATION. Grow in any well-drained, but not dry, soil, preferably in partial shade. Plant and propagate by division in spring.

RECOMMENDED. *H. macra*, *H.m.* Alboaurea, *H.m.* Albo-variegata, *H.m.* Aureola.

 Hakonechloa macra Aureoloa

Halimium

A genus of 14 species of evergreen shrubs thatresemble *Cistus*, but are more botanically related to *Helianthemum*. The soft, silvery foliage blends well with the spring flowers, the petals of which have brown or purple spots at the base.

CULTIVATION. Grow in well-drained soil in a sunny, sheltered site. Protect from severe weather as the plants may be killed back to ground level.

RECOMMENDED. *H. halimifolium*, *H. lasianthum*, *H.l. formosum*, *H. ocymoides*, *H.o.* Concolour, *H. umbellatum.*

Halimium ocymoides

Hebe

A genus of 100 species of evergreen shrubs and trees with small, tubular-based flowers. The genus is split into two groups; those with elliptic to linear leaves and those with tiny scale leaves. Known to be a tender species, some will need protection from freezing weather. Most species are hardy except in areas of prolonged winter cold.

CULTIVATION. Grow in any ordinary, well-drained soil, preferably in humus-rich in sunny sites, the half-hardy types against walls or in sheltered places. Light shade is tolerated by the larger-leaved species and cultivars. Plant autumn to spring. Propagate by cuttings of non-flowering shoots any time from late spring to autumn. Seed may be sown in spring under glass, but as the species hybridize freely, plants may not come true.

RECOMMENDED. *H. albicans, H.* x *andersonii, H.* x *a.* Midsummer Beauty, *H.* x *a.* Variegata, *H. armstrongii, H. ochracea, H.* x Autumn Glory, *H.* x Bowles, *H. brachysiphon, H.b.* White Gem, *H. buchananii, H.b.* Minor, *H.* x Carl Teschner, *H. cupressoides, H.* x Edinensis, *H. elliptica, H. epacridea, H.* x *franciscana* Blue Gem, *H.* x *F.* Variegata, *H. glaucophylla, H.g.* Variegata, *H.* x Great Orme, *H. hectori, H. hulkeana, H. maracantha, H. ochracea, H. odora, H. pinguifolia, H.p.* Pagei, *H. propinqua, H. rakaiensis, H. recurva, H.r.* Aoira, *H. salicifolia, H. speciosa, H.s.* Alicia Amhurst, *H.s.* Gauntlettii, *H. subalpina.*

▼ *Hebe speciosa* Gauntlettii

Hedera

A genus of 5–15 species of evergreen climbers that have both climbing and non-climbing stems, the latter bearing short, adhesive roots. The 5-petalled flowers are small and greenish followed by blackish berries.

CULTIVATION. Grow in any well-drained soil in sun or shade, providing support on trees or walls. Good ground cover species for shady sites. Plant autumn or spring. Propagate by cuttings spring to early autumn.

RECOMMENDED. *H. colchica, H. helix.*

Hedera helix Goldheart ▶

Helenium

A genus of 40 species of annuals and herbaceous perennials. Generally one species and its hybrid cultivars are available. Colours vary from yellow to orange-yellow to orange-brown.

CULTIVATION. Grow in well-drained, moisture-retentive soil in a sunny site. Plant autumn to spring. Propagate by division at planting time.

RECOMMENDED. *H. autumnale, H. bigelovii, H. Bruno, H. Butterpat, H. Coppelia, H. Pumilum.*

◀ *Helenium autumnale*

Helianthemum

A genus of 100 species of annuals, perennials and small shrubs. The widely-open flowers are 5-petalled like small, single roses.

CULTIVATION. Grow in well-drained but moisture-retentive, soil in a sunny site. Plant in spring or autumn. Propagate by cuttings with a heel in summer, overwintering in a cold frame or seed in spring.

RECOMMENDED. *H. apenninum, H. Ben Hope, H. Jubilee, H. lunulatum, H. nummularium, H. opelandicum, H.o. alpestre, H. Wisley Primrose.*

Helianthemum o. alpestre Serpyllifolium ▶

Helianthus

A genus of 110–150 species of annuals and herbaceous perennials that may be fibrous-rooted, tuberous or rhizomatous. Forming clumps or colonies of branched stems and daisy-like flowers, usually in shades of yellow.

CULTIVATION. Grow in any well-drained, moist soil, in a sunny site. Plant perennials autumn to spring, propagating by division at the same time. Sow seed of annuals *in situ* in spring.

RECOMMENDED. *H. annuus*, *H. atrorubens*, *H. deblis*, *H. x multiflorus*, *H. salicifolius*.

◀   *Helianthus annuus*

Helichrysum

A genus of 300–500 species of annuals and perennials. Tufted or clump-forming habit. The flowerheads are disc florets and popular in dried flower arrangements. All are hardy or half-hardy.

CULTIVATION. Grow in well-drained soil in sun, tender species in shelter. Plant in spring, hardy kinds also in autumn. Propagate shrubby and perennial types by cuttings, clump-forming also by division.

RECOMMENDED. *H. bellidioides*, *H. bracteatum*, *H. coralloides*, *H. italicum*, *H. marginatum*.

Helichrysum bellidioides   ▶

Heliopsis

A genus of 12 species of annuals and perennials. One species, its form and cultivars are generally available. Clump-forming with slender-pointed toothed leaves. Flower-heads are yellow, appearing in autumn and can be double or single.

CULTIVATION. Grow in any well-drained, moist soil, in a sunny site. Plant perennials autumn to spring, propagating by division at the same time. Sow seed of annuals *in situ* in spring.

RECOMMENDED. *H. helianthoides*, *H.h. scrabra*, *H.h.s.* Gigantea, *H.h.s.* Golden Plume.

◀   *Heliopsis helianthoides scabra* Golden Plume

Helipterum

A genus of 60–90 species of annuals, perennials, sub-shrubs and shrubs. The plants have simple leaves and flower-heads similar in structure to *Helichrysum*.

CULTIVATION. Plant perennials in spring or autumn. Sow annuals *in situ* in ordinary soil towards the end of spring or raise under glass in mid-spring, planting out in early summer.

RECOMMENDED. *H. albicans*, *H. anthemoides*, *H. roseum*.

Helipterum albicans ▶

Helleborus

A genus of 20 species of evergreen and deciduous shrubs. There are two distinct groups: 1. clump-forming; 2. tufted, shrub-like plants. The flowers are bowl-shaped or flat with 5–6 petals.

CULTIVATION. Grow in any well-drained, limy, preferably humus-rich soil in sun or light shade. Plant in autumn or after flowering. Propagate by careful division immediately after flowering or from seed.

RECOMMENDED. *H. atrorubens*, *H. foetidus*, *H. lividus*, *H. niger*, *H. orientalis*, *H. viridis*.

◀ *Helleborus orientalis* hybrid

Hemerocallis

A genus of 15-20 species of herbaceous perennials that are clump-forming, with arching, linear leaves. The terminal cluster of flowers are lily-like and funnel-shaped.

CULTIVATION. Grow in any ordinary soil, preferably humus-rich, in sun. Plant autumn or spring. Propagate by division at planting time or from ripe seed.

RECOMMENDED. *H. fulva*, *H. lilioasphiodelus*, *H. middendorffii*, *H. minor*, *H. nana*.

Hemerocallis fulva ▶

Hepatica

A genus of about 10 species of tufted perennials. They are closely related to the *Anemone*, but differ in having long-stalked, 3–5 lobed, evergreen leaves.

CULTIVATION. Grow in sun in any well-drained soil, preferably enriched with leaf mould. Plant in autumn. Propagate by division at planting time or from ripe seed.

RECOMMENDED. *H. noblis, H. transsilvanica.*

 Hepatica transsilvanica

Heracleum

A genus of 70 species of biennials and perennials. The leaves are tufted and the tiny, 5-petalled flowers appear as flat umbels. There can be a risk of skin irritation if stem sap gets onto the skin.

CULTIVATION. Grow in ordinary soil in sun or partial shade. Plant in autumn or spring. Propagate from seed. Sow biennials *in situ*. Perennials may be carefully divided in spring.

RECOMMENDED. *H. mantegazzianum, H. minimum, H.m. roseum.*

Heracleum mantegazzianum

Hesperis

A genus of about 30 species of biennials and perennials, with one species being generally available. Also known as sweet rocket. One of the most popular of the scented stocks. Flowers can be single or double.

CULTIVATION. Grow in humus rich soil in sun or shade. Plant in early autumn or soon afterwards. Propagate by separating offsets when dormant or division of clumps at flowering time.

RECOMMENDED. *H. matronalis, H.m.* Candidissima.

 Hesperis matronalis

Heuchera

A genus of 30–50 species of evergreen perennials. The rounded, long-stalked leaves are accompanied by mainly leafless stems. The flowers are small and 5-petalled.

CULTIVATION. Grow in any well-drained, humus-rich soil in sun or light shade. Plant after flowering, autumn or spring. Propagate by division at planting time or from seed in spring.

RECOMMENDED. *H. americana*, *H.* x *brizoides*, *H. cylindrica*, *H. micrantha*, *H. sanguinea*, *H. villosa*.

 Heuchera Red Spangles

Hibiscus

A genus of 250 species of annuals, perennials, shrubs and trees from the tropics and subtropics. They have deeply lobed leaves and the 5-petalled flowers are widely funnel-shaped.

CULTIVATION. Grow hardy shrubs, perennials and half-hardy annuals in well-drained soil in sun. Tender species should be grown under glass. Propagate hardy shrubs and perennials in autumn or spring, half-hardy annuals from seed.

RECOMMENDED. *H. grandiflorus*, *H. moscheutos*, *H. sinosyriacus*, *H. syriacus*, *H. trionum*.

Hibiscus trionum ▶

Hieracium

A genus of 700–1000 species of perennials. The leaves are tufted, often woolly and hairy and the flower-heads consist of tiny petals. This can be an invasive species and is best dead-headed to prevent seeding.

CULTIVATION. Grow in any well-drained soil in a sunny site. Propagate from seed or by division in spring.

RECOMMENDED. *H. aurantiacum*, *H. maculatum*, *H. pilosella*, *H. villosum*, *H. welwitchii*.

 Hieracium villosum

Hippophae

A genus of two species of deciduous, spiny shrubs. One species is generally available; *H. rhamnoides*, also known as Sea Buckthorn. The leaves are silvery-scaled and the tiny petalless, flowers appear in clusters in spring. This is followed by rounded, orange fruit.

CULTIVATION. Grow in any well-drained soil in a sunny site. Plant autumn to spring. Propagate by suckers preferably in autumn or from seed sown when ripe.

RECOMMENDED. *H. rhamnoides.*

Hippophae rhamnoides

Hoheria

A genus of 5 species of deciduous and evergreen trees and shrubs. They have coarsely toothed leaves and small, white, 5-petalled flowers, which are similar to those of the Mallow.

CULTIVATION. Grow in well-drained, humus-rich, soil. Evergreens are more tender than the deciduous species. All can be damaged by frosts. Plant spring. Propagate from seed, layering in spring or cuttings with a heel in late summer.

RECOMMENDED. *H. angustifolia, H. glabrata, H. lyalii, H. populeana, H. sexstylosa.*

Hoheria glabrata

Holodiscus

A genus of 8 species of deciduous shrubs, only one is generally available. The branches arch gracefully and bear tiny, creamy-white, 5-petalled flowers in summer.

CULTIVATION. Grow in any well-drained soil in sun or light shade. Plant autumn to spring. Propagate by semi-hard cuttings in late summer or hardwood cuttings in autumn.

RECOMMENDED. *H. discolour, H.d. delnortensis.*

Holodiscus discolour

Hosta

A genus of about 40 species of herbaceous, clump-forming perennials that are grown principally for their dense mounds of large, overlapping lance to heart-shaped leaves. The foliage colour can vary from the cloudy blue-green to yellow-green. The large, long-stalked leaves can be splashed with cream or silver around the outer edges. These leaves are accompanied by nodding, upright, tubular, almost lily-like flowers. This is a species that is well-suited to the shadier spots of the garden where the sculptured, deeply veined leaves can be used to good effect.

CULTIVATION. Grow in moisture retentive, preferably humus-rich, soil, in light shade or sun. Plant autumn to spring. Propagate by division at planting time or from seed in spring.

RECOMMENDED. *H. albomarginata, H. crispula, H. elata, H. fortunei, H.f.* Albopicta, *H.f.* Aurea, *H.* x Honey Bells, *H. lancifolia, H. plantaginea, H.p. grandiflora, H. rectifolia, H. sieboldiana, H.s. elegans, H. tardiflora, H.* Thomas Hogg, *H. undulata, H. ventricosa, H.v.* Aureomaculata, *H.v.* Variegata.

▼   *Hosta fortunei* Aurea

 *Hosta undulata univittata*   ▲ Hosta Thomas Hogg   *Hosta ventricosa* Aurea ▼

Hosta sieboldiana elegans

Hosta fortunei hyacinthnia ▼

Houstonia

A genus of 50 species of small annuals and perennials from USA and Mexico. This plant resembles chickweed and forms dense cushions of bright green leaves.

CULTIVATION. Grow in moisture-retentive soil in light shade. Plant and propagate by division in spring. The hardy species listed below, are tufted and spreading with slender stems and tubular flowers.

RECOMMENDED. *H. caerulea, H. michauxii, H.m.* Fred Mullard.

Houstonia michauxii ▶

Houttuynia

This is a single species of herbaceous perennial with a widely creeping, often invasive, habit. Each year the plant puts forth large, shiny leaves with a red tint margin. The white, fragrant, flowers appear in summer. The variety 'Chameleon' has leaves splashed with red, cream and deep green.

CULTIVATION. Grow in moist soil or by water in sunny, sheltered sites. Plant and propagate by division in spring.

RECOMMENDED. *H. cordata, H.c.* Plena.

◀ *Houttuynia cordata* Plena

Hyacinthus

This is a single species of bulbous plant. The robust, erect stems have strap-shaped leaves in a basal cluster. The flowers are bell-shaped with 6 mauve-purple to blue, fragrant petals.

CULTIVATION. Grow in any well-drained, humus-rich soil in a sunny site. Plant in autumn. Propagate by removing offsets when dormant or from seed when ripe. Plants may be grown in pots or bowls for home decoration. Plant in cool conditions as heat will result in poor-quality flowers.

RECOMMENDED. *H. orientalis* cultivars.

Hyacinthus Salmonette ▶

Hydrangea

A genus of 23–80 species of evergreen and deciduous shrubs, small trees and climbers. The species is similar to the Viburnum with fertile and sterile flowers produced. The small flowers appear on panicles and can vary in size according to species.

CULTIVATION. Grow in well-drained, but moisture-retentive, soil enriched with humus, in partial shade or sun. Mulch each spring with leaf mould and peat. Prune sparingly, removing only dead or stunted branches for most varieties, but some species will benefit from 3 year-old stems being removed near the base annually in spring. Only remove dead flowers at the end of winter. These are plants that should not be allowed to dry out. Plant in autumn or spring. Propagate from seed in spring under glass, cuttings in late summer or by layering in spring. Liquid feed when flower bud clusters show.

RECOMMENDED. *H. anomala, H.a. petiolaris, H. arborescens, H. aspera, H. heteromalla, H. macrophylla, H.m. normalis, H.m. serrata, H.m. normalis, H.m.s. Rosalba, H. paniculata, H.p. Grandiflora, H.p. Praecox, H. quercifolia.*

▲ *Hydrangea m.* Blue Wave   ▼ *Hydrangea panuculata*   *Hydrangea m.* Deutschland ▲

Hypericum

A genus of 300–400 species of mainly perennials, shrubs and small trees, commonly known as St John's Wort. The flowers range from bright yellow to gold in colour. The evergreen, leathery, linear leaves in some varieties can turn a reddy shade in autumn. A good ground cover plant known for its weed suppressing qualities, it is, however, difficult to get rid of. A very undemanding plant to brighten up a shady corner.

CULTIVATION. Grow in well-drained soil in a sunny site, although some shade may be tolerated. Plant autumn to spring. Propagate shrubs by cuttings in late summer, division, where possible, at planting time or seed from spring. Perennials may be propagated by division, cuttings or from seed in spring.

RECOMMENDED. *H. androsaemum, H. balearicum, H. beanii, H.b.* Gold Cup, *H. calycinum, H. cerastoides, H. coris, H. empetrifolium, H. forrestii, H. fragile, H. Hidcote, H. x inodorum, H. x moseranum, H. x m.* Tricolour, *H. olympicum, H. patulum, H. polyphyllum, H. pseudohenryi, H. reptans, H. trichocaulon.*

 Hypericum polyphyllum

Iberis

A genus of 30 species of annuals, perennials and sub-shrubs. The 4-petalled flowers have 2 petals longer than the others.

CULTIVATION. Grow in any well-drained soil in a sunny location. Plant autumn to spring. Propagate from seed *in situ* for annuals; sub-shrubs by cuttings.

RECOMMENDED. *I. amara, I. gibraltarica, I. saxatilis, I. sempervirens, I. semperflorens, I.s.* Little Gem, *I.s.* Snowflake, *I. umbellata.*

◀ *Iberis umbellata*

Ilex

A genus of 400 species of evergreen and deciduous shrubs. They produce clusters of small, 4–6 petalled, white or greenish flowers followed by red berries.

CULTIVATION. Grow in well-drained, moisture-retentive soil in sun or light shade. Plant autumn or spring. Propagate by cuttings with a heel in late summer or from seed when ripe.

RECOMMENDED. *I. aquilfolium, I.a.* Angustifolia, *I. cornuta, I. crenata, I.c* Mariesii, *I. perado, I. pernyi, I.p. veitchii.*

Ilex x *altaclarensis* Camelliifolia

▼ *Ilex aquilfolium* Argenteo-marginata

Ilex x *altaclarensis* Lawsoniana ▼

Impatiens

A genus of about 500 species of annuals, perennials and soft shrubs. Commonly known as bizzie lizzie. A very popular summer, bedding and container plant, suitable for shady areas as well as sunny spots. They do, however, need at least daily watering in extreme heat, preferably more. They have fleshy stems and flat, often hooded 5-petalled, flowers. Varieties available include dwarf and the taller New Guinea, which has variegated leaves.

CULTIVATION. Sow seed of half-hardy annuals and tender perennials used for summer bedding in mid spring, harden off in early summer and plant out when all danger of frost has passed. Grow hardy annuals in moisture-retentive soil in a sunny site and propagate by sowing seed *in situ* in spring.

RECOMMENDED. *I. balsamina, I.b.* Camellia-flowered, *I.b. glandulifera, I. wallerana, I.w. petersiana.*

 *Impatiens wallerana* Mixed Imp

Incarvillea

A genus of 10 or more species of perennials and annuals from Asia. They have a tufted to clump-forming habit. Flowers are funnel-shaped.

CULTIVATION. Grow in well-drained, humus-rich soil in sun or light shade. Plant in spring. Propagate from seed under glass, in spring or by division.

RECOMMENDED. *I. delavayi, I.mairei, I.m. grandiflora.*

 Incarvillea delavayi

Inula

A genus of 100–200 species of annuals and perennials. Most are clump-forming, mostly with erect stems, bearing daisy-like flower-heads with numerous, yellow florets.

CULTIVATION. Grow in moisture-retentive, but well-drained, soil, preferably humus-enriched. Plant autumn to spring. Propagate by division and from seed in spring.

RECOMMENDED. *I. acaulis, I. ensifolia, I. glanulosa, I. helenium, I. hookeri, I. magnifica, I. orientalis, I. royleana.*

Inula hookeri ▶

Ionopsidium

A genus of one annual from Portugal. The leaves are dense and long-stalked. The solitary flowers are 4-petalled lilac to white and bloom summer to winter.

CULTIVATION. Grow in moisture retentive, well-drained soil in partial shade. Sow seed *in situ*, in spring for summer flowering, in summer for autumn blooming, in autumn for a spring display.

RECOMMENDED. *I. acaule.*

 Ionopsidium acaule

Ipheion

A genus of several species of bulbs from South America with one species generally available: *I. uniflorum*. A tufted, pale to greyish-green leaved plant that can smell of onions when bruised. The star-shaped, solitary flowers are a milky-blue when they appear in spring.

CULTIVATION. Grow in any well-drained soil in a sunny site. Plant in autumn. Propagate by separating the freely produced offsets when dormant or seed in spring.

RECOMMENDED. *I. uniflorum*, *I.u.* Wisley Blue.

Ipheion uniflorum ▶

Ipomoea

A genus of about 500 species of climbing and erect annuals, perennials and shrubs. The species recommended are twining climbers with tubular funnel-shaped flowers.

CULTIVATION. All species can be grown outside in summer, in humus-rich, sunny sites or under glass. Sow seed in spring. Support with sticks.

RECOMMENDED. *I. acuminata*, *I. bona-nox*, *I. coccinea*, *I, hederacea*, *I. nil*, *I. purpurea*, *I. quamoclit*, *I. rubrocaerulea*, *I. tricolour*, *I.t.* Flying Saucers, *I.t.* Heavenly Blue.

◀ *Ipomoea acuminata*

Iresine

A genus of 70–80 species of perennials and sub-shrubs, some climbing. A few species are grown as bedding or house plants. The tiny flowers are white to greenish and usually removed to promote leafy growth.

CULTIVATION. Grow in a greenhouse in light shade with humidity in summer. Propagate by cuttings in spring and harden off in early summer.

RECOMMENDED. *I. herbstii*, *I.h.* Aureo-reticulata, *I. lindenii*.

Iresine herbstii Aureo-reticulata ▶

Iris

A genus of up to 300 species of rhizomatous or bulbous perennials from the northern temperate zone. They are tufted or clump-forming with sword-like leaves and showy, 6-petalled tubular-based, solitary or clustered flowers. The fruits are capsules containing spherical to flattened seed, capable of distribution by water, wind or animals. The genus splits into two distinct groups and within these divisions there are a number of groups each having similarities.

There is a bearded, hybrid species within the two distinct groups. This compromises a vast complex group of cultivars and embraces all the colours of the rainbow. There are three divisions based on height; tall, medium and dwarf. The colours fall into a code of: *Amoena*, standard white; *Bicolour*, flowers one colour, standards a lighter shade; *Blend*, several colours in various combinations; *Plicata*, white or yellow colour stippled, speckled, feathered around the margins with other colours; *Self*, all the same colour; *Variegata*, yellows, golds and oranges either veined or pure colour, with a contrasting colour, usually a shade of brown or red.

CULTIVATION. Irises generally thrive in ordinary soil in sunny or lightly shaded sites, but each variety has its own requirements. Plant rhizomatous species autumn to spring, the bearded types ideally after flowering; bulbous ones in early autumn. All the smaller irises make good pot plants for the alpine house or cool greenhouse. Propagate from seed when ripe, during the autumn or spring and by division or offsets at planting time.

RECOMMENDED. *I. bakerana, I. bucharica, I. chamaeiris, I.c.* Rubella, *I. clarkei, I. cristata, I. dandordiae, I. douglasiana, I. foetidissima, I. forrestii, I. germanica, I. gracilipes, I. graminea, I. innominata, I. kaempferi* cultivar, *I. laevigata* cultivar, *I. pallida, I. pseudacorus* Variegata, *I. pumila* Blue Denim, *I. pumila* Pogo, *I. reticulata, I. sanguinea, I. setosa, I. sibirica, I, spuria, I. tectorum, I. tenax, I. tuberosa, I. uniguicularis, I. vartsnii, I. verna, I. versicolour, I. winogradowii, I. xiphioides, I. xiphium.*

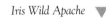
Iris danfordiae

Iris Wild Apache ▼

▲ *Iris xiphium* cultivar   ▼ *Iris pallida* Aurea-variegata   *Iris kaempferi* cultivar ▲

Jasminum

A genus of 200–300 species of deciduous and mainly tropical evergreen shrubs and climbers. with simple leaves. The flat, tubular flowers have 4–9 petals, followed by black berries.

CULTIVATION. Grow in well-drained, but moisture-retentive, soil in sun or light shade. Plant autumn or spring and provide support for twining varieties. Propagate by cuttings in late summer or early autumn.

RECOMMENDED. *J. beesianum, J. humile, J. mesnyi, J. nudiflorum, J. officinale, J. polyanthum.*

◀ *Jasminum polyanthum*   *Jasminum mesnyi* ▼

Jovellana

A genus of 7 species of perennials and sub-shrubs. They have helmet or bell-like, 2-lipped flowers. One species is generally available; *J. violacea.* This is a sub-shrub with coarse leaves and pale violet-purple flowers, spotted purple within.

CULTIVATION. Plant hardy sorts in well-drained, but moisture-retentive, soil in sun or light shade. Grow tender species in pots. Raise annuals under glass. Propagate shrubby species by cuttings in summer or spring.

RECOMMENDED. *J. violacea.*

◀ *Jovellana violacea*

Kerria

A genus of one deciduous, suckering shrub with twiggy, green stems. The flowers are 5-petalled, golden-yellow and appear with the first leaves in spring through to summer.

CULTIVATION. Grow in well-drained, but not dry, soil in a sunny or shady site. Plant autumn to spring. Propagate by division or suckers or cuttings of young shoots with a heel.

RECOMMENDED. *K. japonica*, *K.j.* Pleniflora, *K.j.* Aureo-variegata, *K.j.* Picta, *K.j.* Simplex.

 Kerria japonica Pleniflora

Kniphofia

A genus of 60–75 species of mainly evergreen perennials. They have a clump-forming or tufted habit on a short, trunk-like stem. The flowers are pendant, tubular and alter in colour from reddish to yellow with age.

CULTIVATION. Grow in well-drained, but moisture-retentive, soil in sun. Protection may be needed in cold areas. Plant in spring. Propagate by division or from seed in spring.

RECOMMENDED. *K. caulescens*, *K. galpinii*, *K. modesta*, *K. northiae*, *K. pumila*, *K. tuckii*.

Kniphofia galpinii

Kochia

A genus of 80–90 species of annuals, perennials and sub-shrubs. One species is commonly grown; *K. scoparia*, a half-hardy annual. This has a columnar or pyramidal habit with bright green leaves and tiny green flowers.

CULTIVATION. Grow in fertile, well-drained soil in sun. Sow seed in mid-spring. Seed can also be sown *in situ* late spring to early summer.

RECOMMENDED. *K. scoparia*, *K.s.* trichophylla, *K.s.t.* Childisii.

 K.scoparia trichophylla Childissii

Lamium

A genus of 40–50 species of annuals and perennials. They have a tufted or clump-forming habit, often spreading widely. The flowers are tubular with one, hooded petal.

CULTIVATION. Grow in any well-drained soil in sun or partial shade. Plant autumn to spring. Propagate by division at planting time or from seed in spring.

RECOMMENDED. *L. garganicum, L. maculatum, L.m.* Album, *L.m.* Aureum, *L.m.* Roseum, *L. orvala.*

Lamium maculatum Aureum ▶

Lampranthus

A genus of 160 species of succulent perennials and sub-shrubs. They have a prostrate to erect habit with solitary clusters of many-petalled flowers, resembling daisies.

CULTIVATION. Greenhouse plants, or treat as half-hardy annual, except in mild areas where they can be grown outside in sun. Propagate by cuttings in summer or from seed in spring.

RECOMMENDED. *L. haworthii, L. multiradiatus, L. roseus, L. stipulaceua.*

◀ *Lampranthus aurantiacus*

Lantana

A genus of 150 species of evergreen shrubs an perennials. The shrubby species has flat-headed flowers followed by black berries.

CULTIVATION. Grow outside in warm areas or in a well-ventilated greenhouse. If container grown, feed regularly during the summer. Propagate by cuttings in late summer. Seed may be sown in early spring for flowers the same year.

RECOMMENDED. *L. camara, L.c. hybrida, L. montevidensis.*

Lantana camara ▶

Lathyrus

A genus of 100–150 species of annual and perennial, erect and climbing plants, which includes the popular Sweet pea. The flowers are pea-like followed by slender pods of hard, rounded seeds.

CULTIVATION. Grow in well-drained, humus-rich soil in a sunny site. For Sweet peas add 1–2 buckets of well-decayed manure and bonemeal. Plant perennials autumn to spring and propagate by division or from seed at the same time.

RECOMMENDED. *L. latifolius, L. odoratus, L.o. nanellus, L. rotundifolius, L. vernus.*

Lathyrus odoratus cultivars ▶

Lavandula

A genus of about 20 species of evergreen shrubs and sub-shrubs with dense spikes of fragrant, tubular, 2-lipped flowers. A very traditional cottage garden specimen and dried flower.

CULTIVATION. Grow in any well-drained soil in full sun; some species require shelter. Plant spring. Propagate by cuttings in late summer, or from seed in spring under glass.

RECOMMENDED. *L. angustifolia, L.a, alba, L.a. Hidcote, L.a.* Loddon Pink, *L.a.* Munstead, *L.a. vera, L. dentata, L. lanata, L. stoechas.*

◀ *Lavandula angustifolia* Munstead

Lavatera

A genus of 20–25 species of annuals, biennials, perennials and shrubs. They have a mainly erect habit with 5-petalled flowers.

CULTIVATION. Grow in any well-drained soil in a sunny site. Plant perennials or shrubs in autumn or spring. Propagate perennials by division or cuttings in spring, biennials from seed in spring, or cuttings in late summer.

RECOMMENDED. *L. arborea, L. cacheniriana, L. olbia, L.o.* Rosea, *L. trimestris.*

Lavatera trimestris Loveliness ▶

Leptospermum

A genus of 40–50 species of evergreen trees and shrubs. They generally have a bushy habit with slender stems and small linear to rounded leaves. The flowers are 5-petalled and either solitary or in clusters. With the exception of *L. humifuscum*, the species listed below require a frost-free, sunny and well-ventilated greenhouse or a sheltered, warm wall with protection in winter in all but the mildest areas.

CULTIVATION. Pot or plant in spring in well-drained soil or a good commercial potting mixture; limy soils should be well-laced with peat. Propagate by cuttings with a heel in late summer, or from seed in spring.

RECOMMENDED. *L. flavescens*, *L.f. obovatum*, *L. humifusum*, *L. lanigerum*, *L.l. cunninghamii*, *L. scoparium*, *L.s.* Chapmanii, *L.s.* Keatleyi, *L.s. nanum*, *L.s.* Nichollsii, *L.s.* Red Damask.

▼ *Leptospermum lanigerum cunninghamii*

Lespedeza

A genus of about 100 species of shrubs, sub-shrubs, perennials and annuals. The large, vigorous branches arch over in summer, bearing rosy-purple flowers in autumn and resemble sweet peas.

CULTIVATION. Grow in humus-rich, well-drained soil in sun. Protect from cold and wet conditions. Cut back all stems to ground level in spring and flowers are borne on current season's growth. Plant in spring. Propagate from seed or by division in spring.

RECOMMENDED. *L. bicolour*, *L. thunbergii*.

◀ *Lespedeza thunbergii*

Leucogenes

A genus of 2 species of dwarf, woody-based, evergreen, alpine perennials from New Zealand. They are tufted and form loose to dense mats with silvery, hairy leaves. An alternative version of edelweiss.

CULTIVATION. Grow in a sheltered, sunny scree or dry wall. Plant or pot in spring, adding in grit and peat. Propagate by careful division, from seed in spring or from cuttings in sand late summer.

RECOMMENDED. *L. grandiceps*, *L. leontopodium*.

Leucogenes grandiceps ▶

Leucojum

A genus of 9 species of bulbous perennials. They have strap-shaped leaves and erect, leafless stems bearing several, nodding, snowdrop-like flowers, edged in pale green.

CULTIVATION. Plant in ordinary, slightly heavy soil. Allow the bulbs to become naturalized, forming clumps of increasing size. Propagate from seed when ripe or by offsets separated at planting time.

RECOMMENDED. *L. aestivum*, *L. autumnale*, *L. nicaeense*, *L. roseum*, *L. vernum*, *L.v. carpathicum*.

◀ *Leucojum aestivum*

Leucothoe

A genus of about 45 species of deciduous and evergreen shrubs. They have urn-shaped flowers followed by flattened, rounded, dry capsules. Shade tolerant and an excellent ground cover species.

CULTIVATION. Grow in moist, acid soil incorporating bonemeal in a shady position. Once plants are established, remove old branches to stimulate new leaf growth. This ensures a bushy specimen.

RECOMMENDED. *L. fontanesiana*, *L.f.* Rainbow, *L.f.* Rollissonii, *L. keiskei*.

◀ *Leucothoe fontanesiana*

Lewisia

A genus of 16 species of perennials from the USA that are tufted, rosette-forming and have fleshy roots and leaves. The spreading flowers are brightly coloured and abundant.

CULTIVATION. Position in scree, a dry wall or in vertical rock crevices. Drainage around the neck of the plant must be good to prevent rot during wet weather. Plant in spring. Propagate by division or from seed in spring.

RECOMMENDED. *L. brachcalcyx*, *L. columbiana*, *L. cotyledon*, *L.c. howellii*, *L. nevadensis*, *L. redivia*.

Lewisia cotyledon howellii ▶

Leycesteria

A genus of 6 species of deciduous and evergreen shrubs. One is generally available; *L. formosa*. This species has arching stems and long, funnel-shaped, white, flushed purple flowers in pendant spikes, summer to autumn.

CULTIVATION. Grow in any well-drained soil in sun or partial shade. Plant autumn to spring. Propagate by cuttings summer to autumn or from seed in spring.

RECOMMENDED. *L. formosa*.

◀ *Leycesteria formosa*

Liatris

A genus of 40 species of herbaceous perennials. Clump-forming, mainly from a cluster of corms or tubers, with narrow leaves and spikes of bell-shaped flower-heads.

CULTIVATION. Grow in any well-drained, but not dry, soil, preferably humus-rich, in sun. Plant autumn to spring. Propagate by division at planting time or from seed in spring.

RECOMMENDED. *L. pycnostachya, L. scariosa, L. spicata, L. s. montana. L.s.m.* Kobold.

Liatris spicata montana Kobold ▶

Libertia

A genus of 12 species of evergreen perennials with sword-shaped leaves in fan-like clusters. The erect, wiry stems bear 3-petalled flowers followed by yellow or orange-tinted seed capsules.

CULTIVATION. Grow in well-drained, but moisture-retentive, soil in sun or shade. Plant in spring. Propagate by division after flowering or spring or from seed when ripe. Severe frosts can cause damage so protect with straw or leaves in winter.

RECOMMENDED. *L. formosa, L. grandiflora, L. ixoides.*

◀ *Libertia formosa*

Ligularia

A genus of 80–150 species of herbaceous perennials. Clump-forming with large basal, palmate leaves and erect stems bearing flowers in spring. A good ground cover species for moist soils.

CULTIVATION. Plant in autumn or spring and mix in compost and peat to lighten and improve the soil. Propagate by division at planting time or from seed in spring. Protect from slugs and water regularly.

RECOMMENDED. *L. dentata, L.d.* Desdemona, *L. przewalskii, L. stenocephala, L.s.* The Rocket.

Ligularia dentata ▶

Lilium

A genus of 80 species of bulbous plants producing erect stems that bear narrow, leaves and funnel-, trumpet, bowl, star and turban-shaped flowers. These make fine pot plants for the cold or cool greenhouse.

CULTIVATION. Grow in a well-drained, but not dry, humus-rich soil in sun or partial shade. Some species require acid soil. Protect from extreme heat. Plant in spring except the Madonna lily, which should be planted in summer. Propagate by division when dormant.

RECOMMENDED. Species: *L. amabile*, *L. bulbiferum*, *L. chalcedonicum*, *L. davidii*, *L. formosanum*, *L. hansonii*, *L. henryi*, *L. longiflorum*, *L. martagon*, *L. parda*, *L. pumilum*, *L. regale*, *L. speciosum*. Hybrids: American, Asiatic, Candidum, Martagon, Longiflorum, Oriental, Trumpet, Trumpet types.

Lilium pardalinum   *Lilium candidum*

Lilium canadense

Limonium

A genus of 150–300 species of annuals, perennials and sub-shrubs. Tufted or clump-forming and bearing wiry stems of small spikelets of flowers.

CULTIVATION. Grow in well-drained soil in sun. Plant perennials autumn or spring. Sow annuals *in situ* in late spring. Plants can also be grown in pots. Propagate perennials from seed or by division in spring.

RECOMMENDED. *L. bellidifolium, L. bonduellii, L. incanum, L. latifolium, L. sinuatum, L. suworowii.*

Limonium sinuatum

Linanthus

A genus of 35 species of small annuals with one species generally available. An erect species with long leaves. The flowers are slender-tubed and pink, lilac and yellow coloured.

CULTIVATION. Grow in well-drained soil in sun or light shade. Sow *in situ* in spring or early autumn in a sheltered position.

RECOMMENDED. *L. androsaceus.*

 Linanthus androsaceus

Linaria

A genus of 100 species of annuals and perennials. They have an erect habit with narrow whorled leaves and the flowers resemble those of the *antirrhinum.*

CULTIVATION. Grow in ordinary, well-drained soil in sun. Plant perennials autumn or spring. Sow seed of annuals *in situ* or under glass in spring. Propagate perennials by root cuttings in winter or spring, or by division at planting time.

RECOMMENDED. *L. alpina, L. dalmatica, L. genistifolia, L. purpurea, L. triornithophora, L. tristis.*

Linaria moroccana mixed strains

Linum

A genus of 200 species of annuals, perennials and shrubs. They are tufted with erect stems and clusters of 5-petalled, wide open flowers.

CULTIVATION. Grow in well-drained soil in sun. Plant spring or autumn. Propagate from seed in spring, annuals *in situ*, or cuttings of non-flowering shoots in summer.

RECOMMENDED. *L. alpinum, L. arboreum, L. flavum, L. grandiflorum. L.monogynum, L. narbonense, L. perenne, L.p. alpinum, L. suffruticosum, L.s. salsoloides, L. usitassimum.*

◀ *Linum narbonense*

Linum perenne alpinum ▼

▼ *Linum* x Gemmell's Hybrid

Linum grandiflorum ▼

Lippia

A genus of 200 species of shrubs and perennials. They can have either a prostrate or erect habit. The small, tubular, 2-lipped flowers can be fragrant in lemon, lilac, pink or white spikes in summer.

CULTIVATION. Grow in well-drained soil in mild, sunny areas or in a frost-free greenhouse. Protection is needed in cold areas. Propagate by cuttings in spring or summer or seed in spring.

RECOMMENDED. *L. canescens*, *L. citriodora*.

 Lippia citriodora

Liriope

A genus of 5–6 species of evergreen perennials that are either clump-forming or rhizomatous in habit, with grassy, leathery leaves. The flowers are bell-shaped and followed by berry-like, black fruit.

CULTIVATION. Grow in well-drained, humus-rich soil. Propagate by division in spring or seed when ripe.

RECOMMENDED. *L. graminifolia*, *L. muscari*, *L.m.* Majestic.

Liriope muscari

Lithospermum

A genus of 44 species of annuals, perennials and sub-shrubs with an erect to prostrate habit. The leaves are linear and the flowers are tubular to funnel-shaped. The fruit is formed of 4 nutlets.

CULTIVATION. Grow in well-drained, preferably humus-rich soil in sun or very light shade. Plant autumn to spring. Not reliable in cold, wet areas. Propagate by seed in spring or cuttings in summer.

RECOMMENDED. *L. diffusum*, *L.d.* Grace Ward, *L.d.* Heavenly Blue, *L. oleifolium*.

 *Lithospermum diffusum*

Lobelia

A genus of over 350 species of annuals, perennials, shrubs and trees. They have linear leaves and tubular flowers with petals of differing sizes.

CULTIVATION. Grow half-hardy species in well-drained, humus-rich soil in a sunny sheltered site. Half-hardy species need protection in winter. Grow hardy perennials in moisture-retentive soil in sun or partial shade. Plant in spring. Propagate from seed under glass.

RECOMMENDED. *L. cardinalis, L. erinus, L. x gerardii, L. linnaeoides, L. siphilitica, L. splendens, L. tenuior.*

▲ *Lobelia splendens* Jean

Lobelia erinus Cambridge Blue ▼

▼ *Lobelia cardinalis*

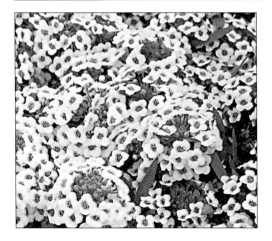

Lobularia

A genus of 5 species of annuals and perennials. One is commonly grown; *L. maritima*, commonly known as sweet alyssum. An annual or short-lived perennial with slender, spreading leaves. The 4-petalled flowers are white and appear summer to autumn.

CULTIVATION. Grow in any well-drained soil in sun or partial shade. Sow *in situ* in spring and plant out in late spring.

RECOMMENDED. *L. maritima, L.m.* Little Dorrit, *L.m.* Violet Queen, *L.m. minimum.*

◀ *Lobularia maritima* Little Dorrit

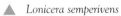

Lonicera pileata   ▲ *Lonicera semperivens*   *Lonicera x americana* ▼

Lonicera

Commonly known as honeysuckle. A genus of 200 species of shrubs and climbers bearing tubular to bell-shaped flowers in terminal spikes or clusters. The flowers are borne in pairs and the fruit may be a single or double berry.

CULTIVATION. Grow in well-drained, moisture-retentive soil in sun or light shade and supported by trellis or wires. Plant autumn to spring. Propagate by cuttings in the late summer or autumn or by seed when ripe.

RECOMMENDED. *L.* x *americana*, *L.* x *brownii*, *L. caprifolium*, *L. etrusca*, *L. fragrantissima*, *L.* x *heckrottii*, *L.* x *h.* Goldflame, *L. henryi*, *L. involucrata*, *L. japonica*, *L.j. halliana*, *L. nitida*, *L. n.* Baggesen's Gold, *L.n.* Ernest Wilson, *L.n.* Yunnan, *L. pericylymenum*, *L.p.* Belgica, *L. pileata*, *L. semperivirens*, *L. syringantha*, *L. tatarica*, *L. tragophylla*.

▲ *Lonicera nitida* Baggesen's Gold

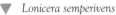 

▼ *Lonicera semperivens*   *Lonicera j. halliana* ▶

Lunaria

A genus of 3 species of annuals and perennials, but only one is generally grown; *L. annua*. Usually biennial, sometimes an annual or short-lived perennial. They have robust stems and bold, toothed leaves. The flowers appear spring to summer in shades of red-purple or white.

CULTIVATION. Grow in any well-drained soil in sun or shade. Sow seed *in situ*, or in a nursery bed, in late spring to early summer; transplant if necessary in autumn.

RECOMMENDED. *L. annua*.

Lunaria annua ▶

Lupinus

A genus of 200 species of annuals, perennials and shrubs. They have palmate leaves and terminal pea flowers that are followed by narrow, flattened pods.

CULTIVATION. Grow in well-drained, moisture-retentive soil, in full sun. Plant perennials autumn to spring. Sow annuals *in situ* in spring or mid-autumn in a sheltered site.

RECOMMENDED. *L. arboreus*, *L. hartwegii*, *L. polyphyllus*.

◀ *Lupinus* Blue Jacket

Luzula

A genus of 80 species of grassy-leaved perennials with a tufted habit and arching, linear leaves. The small 6-petalled flowers are dense and spike-like.

CULTIVATION. Grow in any moderately fertile soil in sun or partial shade. Plant autumn to spring. Propagate from seed when ripe or in spring, or by division at planting time.

RECOMMENDED. *L. nivea*, *L. sylvatica*, *L.s.* Marginata.

Luzula nivea ▶

Lychnis

A genus of 12–35 species of perennials and annuals, closely allied to *agrostemma* and *silene*. Tufted to clump-forming, with erect stems and 5-petalled flowers.

CULTIVATION. Grow in well-drained, fertile soil in sun. Plant perennials autumn to spring, sow annuals *in situ* in spring to autumn. Propagate perennials by division at planting time or from seed sown in spring.

RECOMMENDED. *L. alpina*, *L.* x *arkwrightii*, *L. chalcedonica*, *L. flos-jovis*, *L. viscaria*.

 Lychnis flos-jovis

Lycoris

A genus of 10 species of bulbous plants allied to *amaryllis*. They have strap-like basal leaves that die away just as or before the erect, leafless, flowering stems arise. The 6-petalled, flowers are funnel-shaped.

CULTIVATION. Mainly greenhouse, but some types are more hardy. Bulbs should be protected from frost. Water regularly until leaves yellow, then stop. Propagate from ripe seed or by offsets.

RECOMMENDED. *L. africana*, *L. albiflora*, *L. incarnata*, *L. radiata*, *L. sprengeri*, *L. squamigera*.

Lycoris radiata ▶

Lysimachia

A genus of 160 species of annuals, perennials and sub-shrubs with rounded leaves and solitary flowers. This is a plant capable of flourishing in moist as well as dry conditions, in full sun or partial shade. Also known as loosestrife.

CULTIVATION. Grow in moisture-retentive, deep soil in sun or shade. Plant autumn to spring. Propagate by division at planting time or from seed in spring.

RECOMMENDED. *L. clethroides*, *L. nummularia*, *L. punctata*, *L. vulgaris*.

◀ *Lysimachia punctata*

Magnolia

A genus of 80 species of evergreen and deciduous trees and shrubs. They have large, solitary, goblet-shaped flowers with 6–15 petals.

CULTIVATION. Grow in sun or partial shade in fertile, well-drained but moisture-retentive soil, preferably neutral to acid. Some species can tolerate lime if the site is not too hot and dry and there is plenty of humus. Plant in spring. Propagate by layering in spring or from seed when ripe – this can take 18 months to germinate.

RECOMMENDED. M. *campbellii*, M.c. Alba, M.c. *mollicomata*, M. *delavayi*, M. *denudata*, M. *grandiflora*, M.g. Goliath, M. x *highdownensis*, M. *hypoleuca*, M. *kobus*, M. *lilliflora*, M.l. Nigra, M. x *loebneri*, M. x *l.* Leonard Messel, M. *salicifolia*, M. *sieboldii*, M. *sinensis*, M. *soulangiana*, M. *sprengeri*, M. *stellata*, M.s. Rosea, M.s. Rubra, M. *wilsoniana*.

▼ Magnolia x *soulangiana*

▲   *Magnolia campbellii*   *Magnolia wilsoniana* ▲

▼   *Magnolia liliiflora* Nigra   *Magnolia stellata* ▼

Mahonia

A genus of 70–100 species of evergreen shrubs, closely allied to the *berberis*, but without spiny stems. The leaves are prickly and the flowers appear as terminal clusters.

CULTIVATION. Grow in humus-rich, well-drained soil in shade or sun. Plant autumn or spring. Propagate from seed when ripe. stem tip cuttings in summer, leaf-bud cuttings in autumn, division or suckers or layering in spring.

RECOMMENDED. M. *aquilifolium*, M. *bealei*, M. *japonica*, M. *lomariifolia*, M. *pinnata*, M. *repens*.

Mahonia aquilifolium ▶

 Mahonia x media

Malus

A genus of 25–35 species of deciduous trees and shrubs, commonly known as flowering crab apple. They have rounded, toothed leaves and showy, 5-petalled flowers in spring. These are followed by fleshy fruit in late winter or spring. Named cultivars must be budded or grafted onto seedling domestic apples or one of the specially selected apple rootstocks such as Malling II or Malling-Merton III. In spring, this species is covered with a profusion of pink flowers, clustered tightly against each other. The foliage, which remains after flowering, is attractive in its own right and is joined by brightly coloured fruits in pinks, oranges or reds.

CULTIVATION. Grow in any well-drained, fertile soil, preferably in sun, although light shade is tolerated. Plant autumn to spring. Propagate from seed when ripe, or sown soon after extraction from the fruit in late winter or spring.

RECOMMENDED. M. x *atrosanguinea*, M. *baccata*, M. *coronaria*, M. *dasyphylla*, M. x *domestica*, M. x *eleyi*, M. *floribunda*, M. *hupehensis*, M. x John Downie, M. x *Magdeburgensis*, M. *niedzwetzkyana*, M. *prunifolia*, M.p. *rinki*, M. *pumila*, M. x *p. lemoinei*, M. x *robusta*, M. *sieboldii*, M.s. *sargentii*, M. *spectabilis*, M.s. Riversii, M. *sylvestris*, M. *tschonoskii*.

Malus x *eleyi*

▲ *Malus* x *robusta* Yellow Siberian fruit

Malus x John Downie fruit ▶

Malva

A genus of 30–40 species of annuals, biennials and perennials, commonly known as mallow.

CULTIVATION. Grow in fertile, well-drained soil in a sunny site. Plant perennials autumn or spring, annuals sown *in situ* in spring. Propagate perennials by division or cuttings in spring, biennials from seed in spring or cuttings in late summer.

RECOMMENDED. M. *alcea*, M.*a* Fastigiata, M. *moschata*, M.*m*. Alba.

Malva moschata Alba

Matteuccia

A genus of 3 species of ferns, one of which is generally available; M. *struthiopteris*, commonly known as the ostrich fern. A deciduous perennial that spreads by creeping rhizomes. The fronds arch to form a shuttlecock-shaped rosette.

CULTIVATION. Grow in moist, humus-rich soil in sun or partial shade. Plant autumn to spring. Propagate by division or spores in spring.

RECOMMENDED. M. *struthiopteris*.

 Matteuccia struthiopteris

Matthiola

A genus of 55 species of annuals, biennials, perennials and sub-shrubs. A woody-based stock, grown for its dense spikes of fragrant double flowers which rise from the grey-green, hairy foliage.

CULTIVATION. Grow in well-drained, preferably alkaline soil, in full sun. Sow the seed of hardy annuals *in situ* in spring. Sow seed of perennials and biennials under glass in spring.

RECOMMENDED. M. *incana*, M. *longipetala bicornis*.

Matthiola Brompton strain

Meconopsis

A genus of 43 species of annuals, biennials and perennials that resemble true poppies..

CULTIVATION. Grow in humus-rich, well-drained soil in partial shade and protected from strong winds. Clay or close-textured soil should have grit or peat added. Plant early autumn or spring. Propagate from seed when ripe or under glass in spring. Perennials can be divided or the offsets removed in spring.

RECOMMENDED. M. *betonicifolia*, M. *cambrica*, M. *grandis*, M. *horridula*, M. *integrifolia*, M. *regia*.

◀ *Meconopsis grandis*

Mertensia

A genus of about 45 species of herbaceous perennials with a tufted habit, small leaves and tubular, 5-petalled flowers. The fruits follow are a cluster of 4 wrinkled nutlets.

CULTIVATION. Grow in well-drained, but moisture-retentive, soil in sun or light shade. Plant autumn or spring. Propagate by careful division at planting time.

RECOMMENDED. M. *ciliata*, M. *echiodes*, M. *virginica*.

Mertensia virginica ▶

Milium

A genus of 6 species of annual and perennial grasses. The yellow-leaved form is the species generally available; M. *effusum*, commonly known as golden wood millet. A tufted perennial with arching leaves and nodding spikelets in early to late summer.

CULTIVATION. Grow in well-drained, moist soil, preferably in shade. Plant autumn to spring. Propagate by division or from seed in spring.

RECOMMENDED. M. *effusum*.

◀ *Milium effusum* Aureum

Mimulus

A genus of 100–150 species of annuals, perennials and shrubs with showy, tubular, 5-petalled flowers.

CULTIVATION. Grow perennials in fertile, mois-ture-retentive soil, by water in sun or light shade. Grow shrubs in well-drained soil in a sunny, shel-tered site or in a frost-free greenhouse. Plant in spring. Propagate from seed under glass.

RECOMMENDED. M. *aurantiacus*, M. *cardinalis*, M. *cupreus*, M. *lewisi*, M. *luteus*, M. *moschatus*, M. *puniceus*, M. *ringens*, M. *variegatus*.

◀ *Mimulus aurantiacus*

Mimulus luteus ▼

Mirabilis

A genus of 60 species of annuals and perennials, one of which is generally available; M. *jalapa*. A tender, tuberous-rooted perennial grown as a half-hardy annual. The flowers are fragrant and varied in colour, including striped and open late afternoon through to the morning.

CULTIVATION. Grow in humus-rich soil in a sunny sheltered site or in pots under glass. Sow seed in spring. Plants bedded outside form tubers that can be treated as dahlias.

RECOMMENDED. M. *jalapa*.

◀ *Mirabilis jalapa*

Miscanthus

A genus of 20 species of tall, perennial grasses. The species generally grown are hardy and form bold clumps of broad, grassy leaves topped by feathery spikelets.

CULTIVATION. Grow in moisture-retentive soil in sun or partial shade. Plant autumn or spring. Propagate by division in spring.

RECOMMENDED. M. *saccharifolius*. M. *sinensis*, M.s. Gracillimus, M.s. Variegatus, M.s. Zebrinus.

 Miscanthus sinensis

Mitraria

A genus of one species of evergreen shrub, a root climber, with glossy, deep green leaves. The solitary, pendant flowers are tubular, scarlet in colour and appear early summer to autumn.

CULTIVATION. Cultivate in a frost-free greenhouse or sheltered, shaded site outdoors in mild areas. Grow in a well-drained, moisture-retentive, humus-rich soil. Plant or pot in spring. Propagate by cuttings of non-flowering shoots late spring to autumn or division in spring.

RECOMMENDED. M. *coccinea*.

Mitraria coccinea

Molinia

A genus of 5 species of perennial grasses that are clump-forming, with narrow, arching, small leaves and 2–5 flowered spikelets.

CULTIVATION. Grow in moisture-retentive soil in sun; partial shade is tolerated. Plant spring or autumn. Propagate by division or from seed in spring.

RECOMMENDED. M. *aurundinacea altissima*, M. *caerulea*, M.c. Variegata.

 Molinia caerulea Variegata

Monarda

A genus of 12 species of annuals and perennials. Clump-forming, herbaceous perennials with toothed leaves and dense terminal clusters of tubular, 2-lipped flowers attractive to bees.

CULTIVATION. Grow in moisture-retentive soil in sun or partial shade. Plant autumn to spring. Propagate by division at planting time or from seed in spring.

RECOMMENDED. M. *didyma*, M.*d.* Cambridge Scarlet, M.*d.* Croftway Pink, M.*d.* Mahogany, M.*d.* Snow Queen, M. *fistulosa*.

Monarda didyma Cambridge Scarlet ▶

Muscari

A genus of 40–60 species of bulbous plants with tufted, fleshy leaves. The flowers are urn or bell-shaped and open in spring.

CULTIVATION. Grow in any well-drained soil in sun. Plant autumn. Propagate by offsets or bulblets removed when dormant or from seed when ripe in spring.

RECOMMENDED. M. Argaei Album, M. *armeniacum*, M. *botryoides*, M. *comosum*, M. *latifolium*, M. *macrocarpum*, M. *moschatum*, M. *neglectum*.

◀ *Muscari macrocarpum*

Mutisia

A genus of 60 species of mainly evergreen climbers and shrubs. The terminal, daisy-like flower-heads form distinctive cylindrical or cigar-shaped buds.

CULTIVATION. Grow in well-drained soil in a sheltered, sunny site, preferably among low shrubs. Plant spring, providing a support of twiggy sticks or trellis.

RECOMMENDED. M. *ilicifolia*, M. *oligodon*.

Mutisia oligodon ▶

Myosotidium

A genus of one species of evergreen perennial, commonly known as the Chatham Island lily. Clump-forming in habit, with boldly veined, lustrous, rich green leaves. The flowers are bright blue and appear in spring.

CULTIVATION. Grow outside in mild or cool areas in well-drained neutral to acid soil in a sunny site. Mulch with seaweed. Propagate from seed under glass in spring.

RECOMMENDED. M. *hortensia*.

◀   *Myosotidium hortensia*

Myosotis

A genus of 50 species of annuals and perennials with a tufted and either erect or creeping habit. The leaves are hairy and the tubular flowers are followed by groups of 4 black or brown nutlets.

CULTIVATION. Grow in moisture-retentive, well-drained soil in sun or partial shade. Plant autumn or spring. Propagate from seed in spring, careful division after flowering or spring, or cuttings of non-flowering shoots in summer.

RECOMMENDED. M. *alpestris*, M. *australis*, M. *colensoi*, M. *explanata*, M. *scorpoides*, M. *sylvatica*.

Myosotis australis   ▶

Myrtus

A genus of 100 species of evergreen shrubs and trees with small 4–5 petalled flowers followed by fleshy, often edible, berries.

CULTIVATION. Grow in well-drained soil at the foot of a sunny, sheltered wall. In cold areas, they are best over-wintered in a frost-free greenhouse. Pot or plant spring. Propagate from seed in spring or cuttings with a heel in summer.

RECOMMENDED. M. *bullata*, M. *chequen*, M. *communis*, M. *lechlerana*, M. *luma*, M. *nummularia*, M. *obcordata*, M. *ugni*.

◀   *Myrtus communis*

▲ *Narcissus pseudo-narcissus*

Narcissus Duke of Windsor ▼

▲ *Narcissus* Actaea

Narcissus bulbocodium ▼

Narcissus Texas ▼

Narcissus

A genus of 25–60 species of bulbous perennials. Narcissi have been much hybridized and thousands of cultivars have been named. The best known varieties are the trumpet, large cup, double flowered and small cup. They have strap-shaped or rush-like leaves and leafless stems that bear solitary flowers. Each flower has a tubular base becoming funnel-shaped at the top and terminating in 6 petals. The centre has a trumpet-shaped structure know as a corona. These are followed by a capsule containing polished, black seed. There is a wide variety of this species and they will naturalize themselves quite easily, yellow or white and can emit a soft fragrance.

CULTIVATION. Grow in well-drained soil that is well supplied with water during the growing season, in sun or partial shade. Plant early autumn. Propagate by offsets when dormant or from seed when ripe but this will take 3–5 years to flower. Both species and cultivars make good pot plants for the cool, greenhouse or home. Grow the dwarf species in pans with drainage holes, the large cultivars in pots or bulb bowls. Use a standard potting mixture. Bulb fibre is adequate, but can weaken large, vigorous cultivars so that they do not flower for a year or so. In potting mixture with feeding, they will flower the next year. Pot bulbs as soon as available, placing larger ones with the necks just above the mixture. A combination of too high a temperature and too much wetness or dryness at the roots is the primary cause of failure to flower.

RECOMMENDED. *N. asturiensis, N. bulbocodium, N.b. conspicuus, N. cantabricus, N. cycalmineus, N. jonquilla, N. junctifolius, N. moschatus, N. nanus, N. minor, N. x odorus, N. poeticus, N. pseudo-narcissus, N. romieuxii, N. rupicola, N. scaberulus, N. tazetta, N. triandrus, N. viridiflorus, N. watieri.*

▼ *Narcissus* Fortune

Nemesia

A genus of 50 species of annuals, perennials and sub shrubs, one of which is widely grown; *N. strumosa*, a half-hardy annual. The leaves are coarsely toothed, pale green while the tubular flowers are white, yellow or purple in summer.

CULTIVATION. Grow in humus-rich, well-drained, soil in sun. Sow seed under glass and harden off in early summer, planting out when all fear of frost has passed.

RECOMMENDED. *N. strumosa*.

Nemesia strumosa ▶

Nemophila

A genus of 11 species of annuals. They are slender-stemmed with narrow leaves and 5-petalled solitary, cup-shaped flowers.

CULTIVATION. Grow in well-drained soil in sun. Sow seed *in situ* in spring or in a sheltered site in autumn. They may also be sown under glass in autumn and grown in pots for flowering in a cold greenhouse late spring.

RECOMMENDED. *N. maculata*, *N. menziesii*.

◀ *Nemophila menziesii*

Nerine

A genus of 20–30 species of bulbous plants with a tufted habit. The arching, erect, leaves are strap-shaped and the leafless stems bear 6-petalled flowers in autumn.

CULTIVATION. Mainly a greenhouse species, requiring sun and good ventilation. Some species can survive outside in a sheltered spot. Pot or plant late summer, repotting every 3–5 years. Propagate from ripe seed.

RECOMMENDED. *N. bowdenii*, *N. filifolia*, *N. flexuosa*, *N. masonorum*, *N. sarniensis*, *N. undulata*.

Nerine bowdenii ▶

Nicotiana

A genus of 66 species of annuals and perennials. They have erect, branched stems with long, tubed, 5-lobed flowers what often open fully only after dusk. Grown as half-hardy annuals, but can be grown as pot plants under glass.

CULTIVATION. Grow in humus-rich, well-drained soil in sun, in frost-free areas. Sow seed under glass in spring.

RECOMMENDED. *N. alata, N. forgetiana, N. glauca, N. rustica, N. suaveolens, N. sylvestris, N. tabacum.*

◀ *Nicotiana* Crimson Rocket

Nicotiana alata Sensation Mixed ▼

Nierenbergia

A genus of 30–35 species of perennials and sub-shrubs with a neat, bushy habit, either prostrate or erect. The 5-petalled flowers are funnel or cup-shaped and the leaves are linear.

CULTIVATION. Grow in well-drained soil in sun. Plant in spring. Propagate by cuttings in early autumn or from seed in spring.

RECOMMENDED. *N. hippomanica*, *N.h. violacea*, *N. repens*, *N. scoparia*, *N.s. scoparia*.

Nierenbergia hippomanica violacea ▶

Nolana

A genus of 60 species of mainly fleshy-leaved perennials and sub-shrubs. They have a prostrate habit with linear leaves. The flowers are bell or funnel-shaped followed by woody, fruit capsules.

CULTIVATION. Grow in sharply drained, fertile soil in sun. Propagate from seed in spring in a mixture containing one-third coarse sand. Plant out when all danger of frost has passed.

RECOMMENDED. *N. acuminata*, *N. humifusa*, *N. paradoxa*.

◀ *Nolana paradoxa*

Nomocharis

A genus of 15 species of bulbous-rooted perennials that resemble *lilium* and are closely related. The flowers open saucer-shaped to almost flat and can be fringed.

CULTIVATION. Grow in well-drained, humus-rich soil in sun or partial shade, protected from the midday heat. Plant autumn to spring. Propagate from seed or by scales.

RECOMMENDED. *N. aperta*, *N. farreri*, *N. x finlayorum*, *N. mairei*, *N. oxypetala*, *N. pardanthina*.

Nomocharis aperta ▶

Nymphaea

A genus 30–50 species of aquatics with thick tuberous rhizomes and rounded floating leaves on flexible stalks. The cup-shaped floating flowers have numerous petals, followed by a spongy, berry-like capsule.

CULTIVATION. Grow in water up to 1 m deep in sun or light shade. Ideally grow in a natural mud bottom. Plant in spring. Propagate by division or from ripe seed.

RECOMMENDED. *N. alba*, *N. caerulea*, *N. capensis*, *N.* x *chromatella*, *N.* Escarboucle, *N.* Gladstoniana, *N.* James Brydon, *N. mexicana*, *N.* x *moorei*, *N.* Mrs Richmond, *N. odorata*, *N.o.* Alba. *N.o.* Minor, *N. pygmaea*, *N. stellata*, *N, tuberosa*, *N.t.* Richardsonii.

◀ *Nymphaea* x *chromatella*

◀ *Nymphaea* Escarboucle   *Nymphaea* Sunrise ▼

Oenothera

A genus of 80 species mainly of annuals and perennials. They have linear leaves and 4-petalled, cup-shaped flowers in either solitary or spikes, followed by fruit borne in a capsule.

CULTIVATION. Grow in well-drained soil in sun. Plant hardy species autumn to spring, others in spring. Sow annuals *in situ* in late spring. Plants can also be grown in pots. Propagate all species from seed under glass.

RECOMMENDED. *O. biennis*, *O. caespitosa*, *O. hookeri*, *O. nuttallii*, *O. pallida*, *O. speciosa*.

Oenothera caespitosa ▷

Olearia

A genus of 100–130 species of evergreen shrubs or small trees. They have leathery leaves and terminal clusters of white, small, daisy-like flower-heads. Known to be tender, none of the species will survive a hard winter. All thrive near the sea.

CULTIVATION. Grow in well-drained, moisture-retentive soil in sun. Plant in spring. Propagate by heel cuttings late summer or ripe seed.

RECOMMENDED. *O. albida*, *O. erubescens*, *O. frostii*, *O. ilicifolia*, *O.p.* Splendens, *O. semidentata*.

◁ *Olearia semidentata*

▽ *Olearia ilicifolia*

Olearia phlogopappa Splendens ▽

▲ *Omphalodes cappadocica*

Omphalodes cappadocica Anthea Bloom ▶

Omphalodes

A genus of 24 species of annuals and perennials. Similar to *cynoglossum*, but they are often smaller with relatively larger flowers. The fruit consists of 4 nutlets. A shade tolerant species

CULTIVATION. Grow in well-drained soil in sun. Plant perennials in autumn or spring. Propagate perennials from seed in spring or by division at planting time; biennials from seed late spring or under glass in early spring.

RECOMMENDED. O. *cappadocica*, O.c. Anthea Bloom, O. *linifolia*, O. *luciliae*, O. *verna*, O.v. Alba.

Ononclea

A genus of one species of fern; O. *sensibilis*, commonly known as the sensitive fern. A long-stalked species with solitary, sterile fronds and much smaller fertile fronds. Sensitive to the first frosts of autumn.

CULTIVATION. Grow in moisture-retentive soil in sun or shade. Plant and propagate by division or spores in spring.

RECOMMENDED. O. *sensibilis*.

◀ *Ononclea sensibilis*

Onopordum

A genus of 25 species of biennial plants. They form tiny rosettes then tall, branched stems bearing thistle-like flower-heads.

CULTIVATION. Grow in any well-drained, fertile soil in sun. Propagate by seed ideally sown *in situ* in spring or seed sown in a nursery bed and transplanted with as much root system as possible. Plants may also be raised in containers.

RECOMMENDED. O. acanthium, O. nervosum.

Onopordum acanthium

 Ophiopogon jaburan Vittatus

Ophiopogon

A genus of 10 species of evergreen perennials which have a tufted habit and leathery, grassy leaves. The small, nodding flowers are 6-petalled and bell-shaped, followed by berry-like seed.

CULTIVATION. Grow in well-drained, humus-rich soil in shade. Provide protection from severe cold. Plant or pot in spring. Propagate by division at planting time or from ripe seed.

RECOMMENDED. O. arabicus, O.j. Vittatus, O. japonicus, O.j. wallicha, O. palniscapus.

Origanum

A genus of 15–20 species or perennials and sub-shrubs. They have small, tubular, 2-lipped flowers in crowded spikelets. Some of the species are aromatic.

CULTIVATION. Grow in well-drained soil in sun. Tender species should be given shelter. Plant in spring. Propagate by division at planting time, seed under glass or cuttings in spring.

RECOMMENDED. O. amanum, O. dictamnus, O. hybridum, O. laevigatum, O. pulchrum, O. rotundifolium, O. scabrum, O tournefortii.

Origanum amanum

Ornithogalum

A genus of 100–130 species of bulbous perennials with strap-shaped to linear leaves and erect, starry, 6-petalled flowers.

CULTIVATION. Grow in any well-drained soil in sun. Place tender species in a warm, sheltered site, lift and store in a frost-free greenhouse over winter.

RECOMMENDED. *O. arabicum*, *O. balansae*, *O. nutans*, *O. pyramidale*, *O. saundersiae*, *O. thyrsoides*, *O.t. aureum*, *O. umbellatum*.

◀ *Ornithogalum umbellatum*

Osmanthus

A genus of 30–40 species of evergreen shrubs with leathery leaves. They bear clusters of 4-lobed, tubular flowers that can be followed by berry-like fruit. A moderately hardy species, but protect from prolonged cold weather.

CULTIVATION. Grow in humus-rich, moisture-retentive soil in sheltered sites in sun or partial shade. Plant autumn or spring. Propagate by cuttings with a heel in summer.

RECOMMENDED. *O. armatus*, *O. x burkwoodii*, *O. delavayi*, *O. heterophyllus*, *O.h.* Aureomarginatus.

Osmanthus heterophyllus Aureomarginatus ▶

Osmunda

A genus of 10–12 species of large ferns with a clump-forming habit. Commonly known as the royal fern. All species are deciduous. A protected plant in the wild.

CULTIVATION. Grow in moisture-retentive, humus-rich soil, preferably in partial shade, although *O. regalis* will grow in sun. Propagate by division or spores in spring. Cut back top growth each autumn.

RECOMMENDED. *O. cinnamomea*, *O. claytoniana*, *O. regalis*.

◀ *Osmunda regalis*

Othonnopsis

A genus of 12 species of shrubby, evergreen perennials. One species is generally available; *O. cheirfolia*. The leaves are paddle-shaped with solitary flower-heads in a rich, yellow colour in summer. Not reliably hardy during hard frost,but survives most winters in milder areas.

CULTIVATION. Grow in well-drained soil in sun. Plant in spring. Propagate by cuttings in summer, overwintering the young plants in a cold frame or greenhouse.

RECOMMENDED. *O. cheirifolia*.

Othonnopsis cheirifolia ▶

Oxalis

A genus of 850 species of annuals, perennials and shrubs some bulbous, other succulents. They have long-stalked, leaves that close at night and 5-petalled flowers.

CULTIVATION. Grow hardy plants in well-drained soil in sun or shade. Plant autumn to spring. Propagate by division at planting time, seed in spring or by cuttings of the shrubby sorts in summer.

RECOMMENDED. *O. acetosella, O. bowiei, O. chrysantha, O. laciniata, O. oregana, O. pes-caprae*.

◀ *Oxalis adenophylla*

▼ *Oxalis depressa*

Oxalis pes-caprae ▼

Paeonia

A genus of 33 species of herbaceous perennials and deciduous shrubs. The herbaceous species are clump-forming with large bowl-shaped flowers consisting of 5–10 petals.

CULTIVATION. Grow in well-drained, humus-rich, moisture-retentive soil in sun or partial shade. Plant early autumn or spring. Propagate from seed or by careful division.

RECOMMENDED. *P. delavayi, P. lactiflora, P. lemoinei* Souvenir de Maxime Cornu, *P. officinalis, P. suffructicosa.*

◀ *Paeonia* x *lemoinei* Souvenir de Maxime Cornu

▼ *Paeonia officinalis* Rubra Plena

Papaver

A genus of 50 species of annuals and perennials that have a clump-forming habit. The long leaves bear 4-petalled, bowl-shaped flowers. Each bloom has a crown of many stamens and a central, ribbed stigma.

CULTIVATION. Grow in well-drained soil in sun. Plant autumn or spring. Propagate annuals from seed sown *in situ* in autumn or spring, perennials ideally the same way.

RECOMMENDED. *P. alpinum, P. burseri, P. kerneri. P. nudicaule, P. oriental, P. sendtneri, P. spicatum.*

Papaver oriental King George ▷

Paraquilegia

A genus of 8 species of small, tufted perennials, one of which is usually available; *P. grandiflora*. A densely tufted species with solitary, anemone-like, delicate, nodding flowers mauve-blue or white in colour.

CULTIVATION. Grow in moist scree in sun, in pans of peaty, gritty soil in an alpine house or frame. Plant spring. Propagate by division or from seed when ripe.

RECOMMENDED. *P. grandiflora.*

◀ *Paraquilegia grandiflora*

Parthenocissus

A genus of 15 species of woody, deciduous climbing plants with large, flat leaves and tendrils. The flowers are small, greenish, 5-petalled and followed by grape-like, blue-black to blue berries.

CULTIVATION. Grow in well-drained, but moisture-retentive, soil in sun or partial shade. Plant autumn to spring. Propagate by cuttings in summer in a frame, hardwood cuttings in autumn, layering in spring or from seed.

RECOMMENDED. *P. henryana, P. himalayana, P. inseta, P. semicordata, P. tricuspidata.*

Parthenocissus tricuspidata ▷

Passiflora

A genus of at least 400 species mainly of evergreen, woody or herbaceous climbers. They have twining tendrils and solitary flowers followed by berries that can be edible in some species.

CULTIVATION. Grow in borders, large pots or tubs in any standard potting mixture. Pot or plant in spring, providing support. Prune congested plants in spring. Propagate this species by cuttings in summer.

RECOMMENDED. *P. caerulea, P.c.* Constance Elliott.

◀   *Passiflora caerulea*

Pelargonium

A genus of 250–300 species of perennials and shrubs, also known as geranium or storksbill. They have large, flat leaves accompanied by long stalked clusters of 5-petalled flowers.

CULTIVATION. Grow in pots or as bedding plants, repotting each spring. Water regularly during the growing season. Deadhead to prolong flowering season. Propagate by cuttings or from seed in spring.

RECOMMENDED. *P. captatum, P. crispum, P. x fragrans, P. x hortorum, P. radens, P. zonale.*

Pelargonium x *hortorum* Irene Cal ▶

▼ *Pelargonium* x *hortorum* Mrs Henry Cox

Pelargonium crispum Variegatum ▼

Peltiphyllum

A genus of one species of herbaceous perennial, *P. peltatum*, commonly known as the umbrella plant. This species forms wide colonies with wide leaves that turn bright red in autumn. The long stemmed flowers are 5-petalled, pink or white and appear in spring before the leaves.

CULTIVATION. Grow in moisture-retentive soil or by waterside in sun or partial shade. Plant autumn or spring. Propagate by division at planting time or seed in spring.

RECOMMENDED. *P. peltatum.*

Peltiphyllum peltatum ▶

Penstemon

A genus of 250 species of perennials and sub-shrubs with a tufted, erect habit. The flowers are tubular and generally 2-lipped.

CULTIVATION. Grow in well-drained soil. Not all are fully hardy. Plant autumn or spring. Propagate by cuttings late spring to late summer, division or from seed in spring.

RECOMMENDED. *P. barbatus, P. campanulatus, P. davidsonii, P. eriantherus, P. fruticosus, P. hartwegii, P. isophyllus, P. laetus, P. pinifolous, P. procerus.*

◀ *Penstemon hartwegii*

▼ *Penstemon isophyllus*

Penstemon fruticosus scoleri Alba ▼

Petunia

A genus of 40 species of half-hardy annuals and perennials with a tufted, erect habit. The hairy leaves can be sticky while the flowers can be funnel or salver-scaled.

CULTIVATION. Grow in fertile, well-drained soil in sun or in pots in ordinary potting mixture. Sow seed thinly in spring. Harden off in summer and plant out after frosts.

RECOMMENDED. *P. axillaris*, *P.* x *hybrida*, *P.* x *h*. Happiness, *P.* x *h*. Miss Blanche, *P. inflata*, *P.* x Snowdrift, *P. violacea*.

◀ *Petunia* x *hybrida* Brilliant Mixed

Phacelia

A genus of 200 annuals and perennials with a tufted habit. They are mainly erect plants with linear leaves and beautiful, 5-lobed, tubular flowers that are fragrant and very attractive to bees.

CULTIVATION. Although an easy-going plant, it prefers to be planted directly into the flowering site, in a sunny location, thinning out seedlings. Sow seed in borders, or in the rock garden.

RECOMMENDED. *P. campanularia*, *P. tanacetifolia*.

Phacelia campanularia ▶

Phalaris

A genus of 15 species of annual and perennial grasses. They have linear leaves and dense, flattened, one-flowered spikelets.

CULTIVATION. Grow in any ordinary garden soil in sun, although most perennials will stand partial shade. Plant perennials autumn to spring. Propagate perennials by division, annuals from seed sown *in situ* in spring.

RECOMMENDED. *P. arundinacea*, *P.a* Picta, *P. canariensis*.

◀ *Phalaris arundinacea* Picta

Philadelphus

A genus of 65 species of deciduous shrubs. They are densely branched and produce white, 4-petalled flowers that open in summer from buds of the previous year.

CULTIVATION. Grow in any well-drained, moderately fertile soil in sun, although partial shade is tolerated. Plant autumn to spring. Propagate by suckers at planting time, semi-hardwood cuttings rooted in a cold frame late summer or hardwood cuttings in autumn. Seed can be sown in spring, but seldom comes true to type if collected from garden plants.

RECOMMENDED. *P. coronarius*, *P.c.* Aureus, *P.* x *cymosus*, *P.* x *c.* Bouquet Blanc, *P. delavayi*, *P. lemoinei*, *P.* x *l.* Avalanche, *P.* x *l.* Erectus, *P.* x *l.* Manteau d' Hermine, *P. microphyllus*, *P. pubescens*, *P.* x *purpureomaculatus*, *P.* x *p.* Belle Etoile, *P.* x Sybille, *P.* x *virginalis*, *P.* x v. Virginal.

Philadelphus cornonarius Aureus ▶

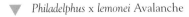
▽ *Philadelphus x lemonei* Avalanche

Philesia

A genus of one species of dwarf evergreen shrub that forms colonies of wiry stems. The dark green leaves are long and narrow. The nodding, 3-petalled flowers are a rose-crimson colour and bell-shaped.

CULTIVATION. Grow in moist, humus-rich, acid soil in shady, sheltered sites. Plant in spring. Propagate by suckers removed in spring.

RECOMMENDED. *P. magellanica.*

 Philesia magellanica

Phlomis

A genus of 100 species of perennials and evergreen shrubs, also known as jerusalem sage. The perennials are clump-forming with velvety, evergreen, broad leaves. The unusual yellow flowers are tubular and hooded.

CULTIVATION. Grow in any well-drained soil in sun, sheltered from cold winds. Plant autumn or spring. Propagate perennials by division and shrubs by cuttings in late summer.

RECOMMENDED. *P. chrysophylla, P. fruticosa, P. italica, P. purpurea, P. russeliana, P. samia.*

Phlomis fruticosa ▶

▼ *Phlomis purpurea*

▲ *Phlomis russeliana*

Phlox

A genus of 60 species of annuals, perennials and sub-shrubs. They have an erect habit and prostrate linear leaves. The 5-petalled, tubular flowers can be solitary or clustered.

CULTIVATION. Grow perennials in humus-rich soil in partial shade, annuals and alpines in well-drained soil in sun. Plant autumn or spring. Propagate by division at planting time, stem cuttings after flowering or root cuttings in spring.

RECOMMENDED. *P. austromontana*, *P. adsurgens*, *P. bifida*, *P. borealis*, *P. caespitosa*, *P. divaricata*, *P. drummondii*, *P. hoodii*, *P. kelseyi*, *P. maculata*, *P. paniculata*, *P. stolonifera*, *P. subulata*.

▲ *Phlox paniculata* Brigadier

▼ *Phlox adsurgens*

Phlox bifida ▼

▼ *Phlox subulata* White Delight

Phlox borealis ▼

Phormium

A genus of 2 species of evergreen perennials with leathery, sword-shaped leaves. The flowers are tubular followed by flattened, black seed.

CULTIVATION. Grow in fertile, moisture-retentive soil in sun; partial shade is tolerated. Liable to damage in severe winters so protect by planting against a wall. Plant in spring. Propagate from seed or by division in spring.

RECOMMENDED. *P. cookianum*, *P. tenax*, *P.t.* Purpureum, *P.t.* Thumbelina, *P.t.* Variegatum.

 Phormium cookianumn Tricolour

Photinia

A genus of 40 species of shrubs and trees with toothed leaves that often flush red in spring or autumn. The 5-petalled flowers are white followed by red, berry-like fruit.

CULTIVATION. Grow in well-drained, humus-rich, moisture-retentive soil in sun or partial shade. Hardy to light frost. Plant autumn or spring. Propagate by cuttings in summer or from seed.

RECOMMENDED. *P.* x *fraseri*, *P. glabra*, *P. serrulata*, *P. villosa*.

Photinia glabra Rubens

Phyteuma

A genus of 40 species of perennials that resemble campanula. The small flowers are borne in tight heads or spikes, each having 5 petals.

CULTIVATION. Grow in well-drained soil in sun, rock crevices or alpine houses. Plant autumn or spring. Propagate from seed when ripe in a cold frame or by division in spring.

RECOMMENDED. *P. comosum*, *P. scheuchzeri*, *P. spicatum*.

 Phyteuma comosum

Pieris

A genus of 8 species of evergreen shrubs with leathery leaves and white, urn-shaped, pendant flowers.

CULTIVATION. Grow in neutral to acid, peaty moisture-retentive soil in sun or partial shade. Provide shelter from strong, cold winds. Not reliably hardy. Plant autumn or spring. Propagate from seed or by cuttings late summer, both in a cold frame.

RECOMMENDED. *P. floribunda, P. formosa, P. japonica, P. nana, P. taiwanensis.*

Pieris Forest Flame ▶

Pimelea

A genus of 80 species of evergreen shrubs, one of which is generally available; *P. prostrata*. This is a a mat-forming species with dense, oblong leaves. The white flowers appear on terminal heads in summer and are followed by berry-like fruit.

CULTIVATION. Grow in well-drained, moisture-retentive soil in sun. Plant autumn to spring. Propagate by cuttings in late spring.

RECOMMENDED. *P. prostrata.*

◀ *Pimelea prostrata*

Piptanthus

A genus of 8 deciduous and evergreen shrubs. One is generally available; *P. nepalensis*. Partially evergreen, this species grows to at least 3m in height. The leaves are dark green and the flowers pea-shaped and bright yellow in colour.

CULTIVATION. Grow in a sheltered, sunny spot in fertile soil. Plant in spring. Propagate from seed under glass in spring, transplanting very carefully to avoid any root disturbance.

RECOMMENDED. *P. nepalensis.*

Piptanthus nepalensis ▶

Pittosporum

A genus of 150 species of evergreen trees and shrubs. They have linear leaves and either clusters of or solitary 5-petalled flowers. The fruit is surrounded by a sticky, bird lime-like substance.

CULTIVATION. Grow in well-drained, moderately fertile soil in a sheltered, sunny site. In colder areas, plant against a wall or in a frost-free greenhouse. Plant or pot late spring. Propagate from seed under glass in spring or cuttings late summer.

RECOMMENDED. *P. crassifolium*, *P. dallii*, *P. eugenoides*, *P. tenuifoloium*, *P. tobira*, *P. undulatum*.

◀ *Pittosporum tobira*

Platycodon

A genus of one species of herbaceous perennial with an erect or clump-forming habit. The stems are erect, bearing toothed leaves and bell-shaped flowers in a deep to pale purple-blue colour.

CULTIVATION. Grow in well-drained, humus-rich soil in sun. Plant autumn to spring. Propagate from seed under glass or by division in spring.

RECOMMENDED. *P. grandiflorus*, *P.g.* Apoyama, *P.g.* Mairesii, *P.g.* Mother of Pearl, *P.g.* Snowflake.

Platycodon grandiflorus Mairesii ▶

Pleione

A genus of 10 species of orchids that have solitary flowers and deciduous, pleated leaves. Most species grow in high mountain forests, on moss-covered rocks, banks and tree trunks.

CULTIVATION. Grow this species in a greenhouse environment, providing light shade in summer. Plant in a peaty mixture including one-third sphagnum moss. Protect from frost and liquid feed during summer months.

RECOMMENDED. *P. bulbocodoides*, *P. yunnanensis*.

◀ *Pleione yunnanensis*

Podocarpus

A genus of 75–100 shrubs and trees. These are conifers with linear, spirally arranged leaves. As the seed develops, in some species, it swells and turns a bright red colour. In other species the seed develops into a plum-like fruit.

CULTIVATION. Grow in well-drained moisture-retentive soil in sun, although partial shade can be tolerated. Plant autumn or spring. Propagate from ripe seed or cuttings late summer.

RECOMMENDED. *P. alpinus*, *P. andinus*, *P. macrophyllus*, *P. nivalis*.

Podocarpus macrophyllus maki ▶

Polemonium

A genus of 25–50 species of annuals and perennials. They have a tufted or clump-forming habit and dense, tubular, 5-lobed flowers.

CULTIVATION. Grow in fertile, moisture-retentive, well-drained soil in sun or partial shade. Some alpine species thrive best in scree. Plant autumn to spring. Propagate from ripe seed or by division at planting time.

RECOMMENDED. *P. caeruleum*, *P. delicatum*, *P. foliosissmum*, *P. jacobaea* Richardsonii, *P. pauciflorum*, *P. pulcherrimum*, *P. viscosum*.

◀ *Polemonium foliosissmum*

Polygala

A genus of 500–600 species of annuals, perennials, shrubs and trees. The leaves are narrow and the flowers resemble those of the pea family.

CULTIVATION. Grow hardy species in well-drained soil in sun or partial shade. Tender species should be grown under glass. Propagate by cuttings in summer for greenhouse species, perennials by division, all others by seed in spring under glass.

RECOMMENDED. *P. calcarea*, *P. chamaebuxus*, *P. c.* Grandiflora, *P. myrtifolia*, *P. vayrede*.

Polygala chamaebuxus Grandiflora ▶

Polygonatum

A genus of 30 species of herbaceous perennials with erect stems and tubular, bell-shaped, pendant flowers. These are followed by blue-black or red berries.

CULTIVATION. Grow in moisture-retentive, humus-rich soil in partial shade, although sun is tolerated. Plant autumn to late winter. Propagate by division at planting time.

RECOMMENDED. *P. commutatum, P. falcatum, P. hookeri, P.* x *hybridum. P. multiflorum, P. odoratum, P. pumilum, P. verticillatum.*

◀ *Polygonatum* x *hybridum*

Polygonum

A genus of 150–300 species of annuals, perennials and sub-shrubs that can be either erect or prostrate in habit. The small, funnel-shaped, flowers are petalless.

CULTIVATION. Grow in any moderately rich soil in sun. Plant autumn to spring. Propagate from seed or by division. Trailing species can be propagated by cuttings in late summer.

RECOMMENDED. *P. affine, P. amplexicaule, P. baldschuanicum, P. campanulatum, P. equisetiforme, P. macrophyllum, P. molle, P. tenuicaule.*

Polygonum affine Donald Lowndes ▶

Polypodium

A genus of 75 species of ferns. One species and its cultivars are generally available. This is a mat or colony-forming species.

CULTIVATION. Grow in moisture-retentive. but not wet, soil in shade. Plant autumn to spring. Propagate by spores or division in spring.

RECOMMENDED. *P. vulgare, P.v.* Bifidum Cristatum, *P.v.* Cambricum, *P.v.* Cornubiensis, *P.v.* Longicaudatum, *P. v.* Pulcherrimum.

◀ *Polypodium vulgare* Pulcherrimum

Poncirus

A genus of one species of deciduous shrub, also known as Japanese bitter orange. The leaves are sparse while the white, fragrant flowers bloom in early summer. The fruit resembles a tiny orange, hence the common name.

CULTIVATION. Grow in mild areas in well-drained, humus-rich soil in sun. Plant autumn to spring. Propagate from seed or by cuttings in late summer.

RECOMMENDED. *P. trifoliata*.

Poncirus trifoliata ▷

Pontederia

A genus of 4 species of aquatic perennials, one of which is generally available; *P. cordata*. A colony-forming species with long, narrow, rich, glossy green leaves. The flowers are funnel-shaped and are blue with yellow spots.

CULTIVATION. Grow in bogs or water in sun. Plant spring or autumn, either in a natural mud bottom, in containers of equal parts loam and decayed manure. Propagate by division at planting time.

RECOMMENDED. *P. cordata*.

◁　*Pontederia cordata*

Portulaca

A genus of 100–200 species of succulent, annual perennials. They have fleshy, linear leaves and flowers with spreading petals that only open in sun. One variety *P. grandiflora* Sundance has double flowers.

CULTIVATION. Grow hardy and half-hardy species in well-drained soil in sun. The seed is fine like dust and should be mixed with sand before sowing *in situ* in late spring.

RECOMMENDED. *P. grandiflora*, *P. oleracea*, *P.o. sativa*, *P.o. sativa* Gigantea.

Portulaca Improved Double Mixed ▷

Potentilla

A genus of 500 species of annuals, perennials and shrubs with a tufted habit and long leaves. The 5-petalled flowers open wide.

CULTIVATION. Grow in well-drained, fertile soil in sun. Plant autumn to spring. Propagate from seed in spring, by division at planting time or cuttings taken in late summer.

RECOMMENDED. *P. alba, P. ambigua, P. aurea, P. cuneata, P. fragiformis, P. fruticosa, P.f.* Berlin Beauty, *P. nepalensis, P. nitida, P. recta. P.r. warrenii, P. tabnaemontani, P.* x *tonguei.*

◀ *Potentilla fruticosa* Red Ace

▼ *Potentilla* x *Elizabeth*

▲ *Potentilla aurea*   *Potentilla* William Rollison ▼

Pratia

A genus of 25–35 evergreen perennials allied to *lobelia*. They have mostly a prostrate habit and erect toothed leaves. The tubular flowers are followed by berries.

CULTIVATION. Grow in moisture-retentive, but well-drained, soil in sheltered, partially shaded or sunny sites. Plant in spring or cuttings in summer.

RECOMMENDED. *P. angulata, P.a. treadwellii, P. macrodon.*

Pratia angulata

Primula

A genus of 400 species of evergreen and deciduous perennials, with an enormous range of sizes and growing habitats. They are tufted to clump-forming and bear tubular flowers.

CULTIVATION. Grow in well-drained, humus-rich soil in partial shade. Mulch with peat. Plant in spring. Propagate by division after flowering and replant immediately.

RECOMMENDED. *P. alpicola, P. auricula, P. beesiana, P. bulleyana, P. denticulata, P. helodoxa, P. japonica* Miller's Crimson, *P. rosea, P. vulgaris.*

◀ *Primula frondosa*

 Primula rosea

Primula marginata ▼

Prostanthera

A genus of 50 species of aromatic, evergreen shrubs. They have linear leaves and tubular 5-lobed, 2-lipped flowers.

CULTIVATION. Mainly a greenhouse species that needs to be grown in well-ventilated conditions with light shade, except in mild areas where it may be possible to grow outside in a sheltered spot. Grow in soil based potting mixture. Plant out in spring. Propagate from seed or cuttings in summer.

RECOMMENDED. *P. cuneata, P. rotundifolia.*

◀ *Prostanthera rotundifolia*

Prunella

A genus of 7 species of evergreen perennials that form low, wide clumps of erect to oblong, deeply lobed leaves. The erect stems bear spikes of tubular, 2-lipped flowers.

CULTIVATION. Grow in moisture-retentive, fertile soil in partial shade or sun. Plant autumn to spring. Propagate by division at planting time or from seed in spring.

RECOMMENDED. *P. grandiflora, P.g.* Alba. *P.g. pyrenaica, P.g. webbiana, P. vulgaris, P.v. rubra.*

Prunella grandiflora webbiana Pink Loveliness ▶

Pulmonaria

A genus of 10–13 species of perennials. They have a creeping habit and form wide colonies. The flowers are funnel-shaped and borne on short stems in spring.

CULTIVATION. Grow in moisture-retentive, humus-rich soil in partial shade, although full sun is tolerated. Plant autumn to spring. Propagate by division at planting time or from seed.

RECOMMENDED. *P. officinalis, P. rubra, P. saccharata, P.s.* Argentea, *P.s.* Cambridge Blue, *P.s.* Pink Dawn, *P.s.* White Wings.

◀ *Pulmonaria saccharata*

Pulsatilla

A genus of 12 species or perennials that are tufted, fibrous-rooted and bear solitary, blue, bell-shaped flowers. The hairy foliage is as attractive as the flowers. A good rock garden specimen.

CULTIVATION. Grow in well-drained, fertile soil in sun. Plant autumn or spring. Propagate from seed when ripe. Old seed germinates erratically.

RECOMMENDED. *P. albana, P. alpina, P. helleri, P. pratensis, P. vernalis, P. vulgaris, P.v.* Alba, *P.v.* Grandis, *P.v.* Rubra.

Pulsatilla vulgaris Alba

Pyracantha

A genus of 6–8 species of spiny, evergreen shrubs. They have small, white, 5-petalled flowers in summer followed by apple-shaped fruit.

CULTIVATION. Grow in any well-drained, moisture-retentive soil. Plant autumn or spring. Propagate from seed or by cuttings with a heel in summer.

RECOMMENDED. *P. angustifolia, P. alatantoides, P. crenatoserrata, P. crenulata, P.* x Golden Charmer, *P. rogersiana, P.r.* Flava, *P.* x *watereri.*

Pyracantha x *watereri*

Pyrus

A genus of 20 species of deciduous trees and shrubs that bear white, 5-petalled flowers that open in spring with the expanding leaves. These are followed by pear-shaped fruit.

CULTIVATION. Grow in any well-drained, fertile soil in sun. Plant autumn to spring. Propagate species from seed and all cultivars should be budded and grafted onto pear or quince rootstock.

RECOMMENDED. *P. amygdaliformis, P. calleryana, P.c.* Bradford, *P. pashia, P. salicifolia, P.s.* Pendula.

Pyrus salicifolia Pendula

Ramonda

A genus of 3 species of evergreen perennials that form flattened rosettes of wrinkled leaves. From these rise several erect stems bearing tubular, 4–5 petalled flowers in late spring.

CULTIVATION. Grow in steeply inclined to vertical rock crevices, dry walls or screes, preferably facing north. Plant autumn or spring. Propagate from seed, by careful division in spring or by leaf cuttings in summer.

RECOMMENDED. *R. myconi, R.m.* Alba, *R.m.* Rosea, *R. nathaliae, R.n.* Alba, *R. serbica.*

Ramonda myconi Rosea

Ranunculus

A genus of 400 species of annuals and perennials with either a tufted or clump-forming habit. They have simple leaves and cup or bowl-shaped flowers formed of 5–15 petals.

CULTIVATION. Grow most species in ordinary garden soil in sun. Alpine species need gritty, humus-rich mixture and aquatics need a mud bottom or loam based mixture. Plant autumn to spring. Propagate from seed or by division.

RECOMMENDED. *R. acris, R. asiacticus, R. bulbosus, R. crenatus, R. ficaria, R. montanus, R. pelatus.*

Ranunculus asiaticus

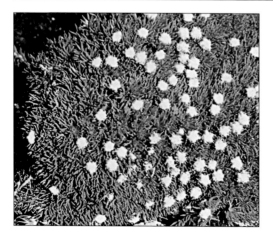

Raoulia

A genus of 25 species of evergreen perennials that are mat or cushion forming in habit. The linear, hairy leaves are accompanied by solitary flower-heads of tiny disc florets.

CULTIVATION. Grow in moist, but sharply drained, soil or screes in sun. Plant or pot in spring. Propagate by division or from seed.

RECOMMENDED. *R. australis, R. glabra, R. hasstii, R. hectori, R. hookeri, R. parkii, R. tenuicaulis.*

Raoulia glabra

Rhaphiolepsis

A genus of 14 species of evergreen shrubs with leathery, glossy, dark green leaves. The 5-petalled flowers are followed by berry-like fruit.

CULTIVATION. Grow in well-drained, fertile soil in a sheltered, sunny site. *R. indica* is best grown in a frost-free greenhouse in large tubs or pots in a good potting mixture. Plant or pot autumn to spring. Propagate from seed under glass or by cuttings late summer.

RECOMMENDED. *R. x delacourii, R. indica, R. umbellata.*

Rhaphiolepsis indica

Rhazya

A genus of 2 species of herbaceous perennials, from Greece to Turkey and Arabia to N.W. India. One form is generally available; *R. orientalis*, a woody-based, clump-forming species.

CULTIVATION. Grow in moisture-retentive, fertile soil in sun or partial shade. Plant autumn to spring. Propagate from seed or by division in spring.

RECOMMENDED. *R. orientalis.*

 Rhazya orientalis

Rheum

A genus of 25 species of herbaceous perennials, with a clump-forming habit and thick, fleshy roots. The large, long-stalked leaves bear erect stems of spike-like, small, 6-petalled flowers.

CULTIVATION. Grow in humus-rich, moisture-retentive soil in sun or partial shade. Plant autumn to spring. Propagate from seed in spring or by division at planting time.

RECOMMENDED. *R. alexandrae, R. nobile, R. officinale, R. palmatum, R.p. tanguticum.*

Rheum alexandrae

Rhododendron

A genus of approximately 800 species of evergreen and deciduous shrubs and trees. Ranging from prostrate mats to large trees, they have leathery leaves and clusters of solitary, tubular, funnel or bell-shaped, 5-8 lobed flowers, often in profusion.

CULTIVATION. Grow the hardy species and cultivars in humus-rich, moisture-retentive, well-drained, acid soil. Large leaved species grow in partial shade, sheltered from strong winds and small-leaved types, in sun or light shade. Half-hardy species need a frost-free greenhouse or warm area. For pot culture use an all-peat acid mix or loam based type, made up with neutral to acid loam and without chalk in the fertilizer. Pot or plant autumn or spring. Propagate from seed in a cold frame or greenhouse in spring, but this method will take several years for the plants to flower. Layering in spring is a quicker method of propagation. Cuttings can be taken in late summer and autumn.

RECOMMENDED. Species: *R. barbatum, R. brachycarpum, R. calophytum, R. falconeri, R. ferrugineum, R. fictolacteum, R. forrestii repens, R. fragrantissimum, R. luteum, R. macabeanum, R. moupinense, R. neri-iflorum, R. orbiculare, R. panticun, R. ponticum, R. schlippenbachii, R. sinogrande, R. thomsonii, R. wardii, R. williamsianum, R. yakushimanum, R. yunnanense.* Cultivars: *R.* x Bambi, *R.* x Britannia, *R.* x Cunningham's White, *R.* x Golden Wit, *R.* x Margaret Dunn, *R.* x Mrs A.T. de la Mare, *R.* x Purple Splendour, *R.* x Sappho, *R.* x Yellow Hammer.

▼   *Rhododendron arboreum*

▲ *Rhododendron barbatum*

Rhododendron calophytum ▲

▼ *Rhododendron ferrugineum*

 *Rhododendron neriiflorum*

▼ *Rhododendron calophytum*

Rhododendron williamsianum ▼

Ribes

A genus of 150 species of deciduous and ever-green shrubs, containing fruit and valuable orna-mental varieties. The stems can be smooth or prickly and the 5-petalled, flowers are bell or tubular-shaped and followed by fleshy berry-fruits.

CULTIVATION. Grow in well-drained, moisture-retentive soil in sun or partial shade. Plant autumn to spring. Propagate from seed, semi-hardwood cuttings late summer or hardwood cuttings in autumn.

RECOMMENDED. *R. aureum, R. laurifolium, R. sanguineum, R. typhina.*

Ribes s. Brocklebankii

Ricinus

A genus of one species of tender, evergreen shrub or small tree; *R. communis*. Also known as the castor-oil plant, grown for its handsome foliage. The leaves are palmate and often bronze to red-tinted, particularly when young. The flowers are petalless and followed by a woody fruit capsule that explodes when ripe.

CULTIVATION. Grow in humus-rich soil in a sheltered, sunny site. Sow seed in spring for planting out when all danger of frost has passed.

RECOMMENDED. *R. communis, R.c.* Cambodgensis.

Ricinus communis cultivars

Robinia

A genus of 20 species of deciduous trees and shrubs with small leaves, also known as false acacia. The foliage is a dense, pale green and the flowers are pea-shaped in summer.

CULTIVATION. Grow in well-drained, fertile soil in sun. In rich soils, stems grow vigorously and are prone to wind damage. Plant autumn to spring. Propagate from seed in spring in a cold frame, suckers at planting time or by root cuttings in late winter in a frame or greenhouse.

RECOMMENDED. *R. hispida, R. kelseyi, R. luxurians.*

Robinia hispida

Rodgersia

A genus of 5–6 species of robust, herbaceous perennials from East Asia. They are clump to colony-forming in habit with long, stalked leaves The small, 5-petalled flowers bloom in summer.

CULTIVATION. Grow in humus-rich, moisture-retentive soil in a sunny or partially shaded site, sheltered from strong winds. Plant autumn to spring. Propagate by division at planting time or from seed in a cold frame.

RECOMMENDED. *R. aesculifolia*, *R. pinnata*, *R.p.* Superba, *R. podophylla*, *R. sambucifolia*, *R. tabularis*.

◀ *Rodgersia aesculifolia*

Romneya

A genus of one species of woody-based perennial from California; *R. coulteri*, also known as California tree or matilija poppy. A spreading species that uses suckers to form colonies or clumps. The flowers are poppy-like, white and fragrant, blooming late summer to autumn.

CULTIVATION. Grow in fertile, well-drained soil in sunny, sheltered sites. Plant in spring. Propagate by root cuttings, seed or by careful division.

RECOMMENDED. *R. coulteri*.

Romneya coulteri

Romulea

A genus of 75–90 species of cormous-rooted perennials that resemble crocus. The flowers are carried well above the ground.

CULTIVATION. Plant in autumn in any standard potting mixture. Water sparingly until the leaves appear, then water more regularly. When leaves start to yellow, dry off. Propagate by offsets at planting time or from seed in spring under glass.

RECOMMENDED. *R. bulbocodiodes*, *R. bulbocodium*, *R. longituba*, *R.l. alticola*, *R. requienii*, *R. rosea*.

◀ *Romulea bulbocodium*

Rosa

A genus of 100–200 species of shrubs and woody climbers. They have toothed leaves, prickly stems and clusters of widely expanded, 5-petalled flowers. The fruit is known as a hip or hep.

CULTIVATION. Grow in well-drained, but moisture-retentive, soil in sun, although climbers are shade tolerant and may be grown up shady walls or trees. Plant autumn to spring. All roses, especially the hybrid tea, floribunda, miniature and rambler types, need regular feeding and/or mulching. An annual mulch of decayed manure or well-made garden compost in spring is ideal. Alternatively, moss, peat or shredded bark can be used with a general fertilizer or use a specially compounded rose fertilizer. Propagate from seed, in the garden or in a cold frame or by hardwood cuttings in autumn. Soft and semi-hardwood cuttings may be taken in late spring or summer. Most cultivar groups need pruning, autumn to spring, but choose mild weather and sharp secateurs.

RECOMMENDED. Species: *R. bracteata*, *R. bulbocodium*, *R. californica* Plena, *R. chinensis*, *R. fedtschenkoana*, *R. foetida*, *R. gallica*, *R. hugonis*, *R. macrophylla*, *R. moyesii*, *R. omeiensis pteracantha*, *R. pimpinellifolia altaica*, *R. primula*, *R. rubrifolia*, *R. rugosa*, *R. villosa*, *R. virginiana*, *R. webbiana*, *R. willmottiae*, *R. woodsii*, *R. xanthina*. Cultivars: *R.* Albertine, *R.* Baby Masquerade, *R.* Blue Moon, *R.* Constance Spry, *R.* Cornelia, *R.* Dorothy Perkins, *R.* Elizabeth of Glamis, *R.* Iceberg, *R.* Mermaid, *R.* Nevada, *R.* Peace, *R.* Pink Perpétue, *R.* Reines des Violettes, *R.* Super Star, *R.* William Lobb.

▼ *Rosa* Pink Perpétue

▲ *Rosa Peace*

Rosa Baby Masquerade ▼

▼ *Rosa* x *paulii*   ▲ *Rosa* Albertine   *Rosa* Dorothy Perkins ▼

Rosa Mermaid ▼

Rubus

A genus of 250 species deciduous and evergreen, often prickly shrubs and scramblers with simple leaves and 5-petalled flowers. The edible fruit is known as raspberry and is rounded to cylindrical in shape.

CULTIVATION. Grow in well-drained, fertile soil in sun or partial shade. Plant autumn to spring. Propagate by division, suckers at planting time, tip-layering or from seed.

RECOMMENDED. *R. arcticus, R. deliciosus, R. phoenicolasius, R. thibetanus, R. tricolour.*

Rubus deliciosus ▶

Rudbeckia

A genus of 25 species of annuals, biennials and perennials from North America. They are sturdy, erect plants with simple leaves and daisy-like flower-heads.

CULTIVATION. Grow in fertile soil in sun or partial shade. Plant autumn to spring. Propagate by division at planting time or from seed.

RECOMMENDED. *R. fulgida, R.f. speciosa, R.f. sul, R.h.p.* Double Gloriosa, *R.h.p.* Superba, *R. laciniata, R.l.* Soleil d' Or, *R. maxima, R. nitida.*

◀ *Rudbeckia hirta* Rustic Dwarfs

Ruscus

A genus of 3–7 species of evergreen shrubs known as broom. Clump-forming or tufted in habit with green stems and small, starry 6-petalled flowers. These are followed by red fruit or yellow berries.

CULTIVATION. Grow in humus-rich soil in shade or partial shade. Plant autumn to spring. Propagate by division in spring or from seed.

RECOMMENDED. *R. aculeatus, R.a.* Hermaphroditus, *R. hypoglossum.*

Ruscus aculeatus ▶

Salix

A genus of 300–500 species of deciduous trees and shrubs with linear leaves and tiny, petalless flowers, packed into catkins. The seed is minute, and bears long, silky hairs for wind dispersal. Some forms have stems used for basket making.

CULTIVATION. Grow in fertile, moisture-retentive soil in sun or partial shade. Plant autumn to spring. Propagate by softwood cuttings in summer or hardwood outside in autumn.

RECOMMENDED. *S. alba, S.a. chinensis. S. apoda, S. daphnoides, S. hastata, S. lanata, S. reticulata.*

◀ *Salix myrsinites* in fruit

Salix alba Chermesina ▼

Salvia

A genus of 700 species of annuals, biennials, perennials and shrubs. They have a mainly erect habit and bear pretty, tubular, 2-lipped flowers.

CULTIVATION. Grow hardy and half-hardy species in well-drained, fertile soil in sun. Plant in spring, the hardy perennials also in autumn. Propagate all varieties from seed in spring, half-hardies under glass, perennials by division, shrubs by cuttings late spring.

RECOMMENDED. *S. argentea*, *S. elegans*, *S. officinalis*, *S. splendens*, *S. x superba*, *S. viridis*.

Salvia splendens ▶

Sambuscus

A genus of 20 species of deciduous shrubs or small trees, commonly known as elder. They have hollow stems and small, white flowers. The fruit is fleshy and berry-like, edible in some species and poisonous in others.

CULTIVATION. Grow in moisture-retentive, well-drained soil in sun or partial shade. Plant autumn to spring. Propagate from seed, by semi-hardwood cuttings or by division at planting time.

RECOMMENDED. *S. canadensis*, *S.c.* Aurea, *S.c.* Rubra, *S.c.* Scotia, *S. nigra*, *S. racemosa*.

◀ *Sambuscus racemosa* Plumosa Aurea

Sanguinaria

A genus of one species of perennial that produces fleshy rhizomes and long stalked, rounded, blue-grey, prominently veined leaves. The flowers are solitary, 8–16 petalled and appear as the leaves are unfurling.

CULTIVATION. Grow in humus-rich, moisture-retentive soil in dappled or partial shade. Plant when dormant, preferably in autumn or immediately after flowering. Propagate by division or from seed.

RECOMMENDED. *S. canadensis*.

Sanguinaria canadensis ▶

Santolina

A genus of 8–10 species of small, aromatic, ever-green shrubs. They have narrow, toothed leaves and button-like flower-heads.

CULTIVATION. Grow in well-drained soil in sun. Plant autumn to spring. Propagate semi-hardwood cuttings in late summer in a cold frame, hardwood cuttings in autumn *in situ*. May be clipped annually to maintain a compact shape.

RECOMMENDED. *S. chamaecyparissus*, *S.c.* Nana, *S. rosmarinifolia*, *S.r.* Primrose Gem.

◀ *Santolina chamaecyparissus* Nana

Sanvitalia

A genus of 7 species of annuals, perennials and shrubs, one of which is generally available: *S. procumbens*. This hardy, annual plant has a creeping habit and forms dense mounds. The flower-heads are daisy-like with broad, black centres in summer to autumn.

CULTIVATION. Grow in fertile, well-drained soil in sun. Sow seed *in situ* autumn or spring, planting out late spring or early summer.

RECOMMENDED. *S. procumbens*.

Sanvitalia procumbens ▶

Sarcococca

A genus of 14 species of evergreen shrubs. The petalless flowers, which are often fragrant, are followed by black or red berries.

CULTIVATION. Grow in any well-drained but moisture-retentive, soil, preferably humus-rich, in partial shade, sheltered from cold winds. Plant autumn or spring. Propagate by cuttings in late summer in a cold frame or from seed. Fairly hardy and can flower in winter.

RECOMMENDED. *S. confusa*, *S. hookeriana*, *S.h. digyna*, *S.h. humilis*, *S. ruscifolia*, *S.r. chinensis*.

◀ *Sarcococca confusa*

Saxifraga

A genus of 350 species of mainly small perennials and a few annuals. They are largely tufted in habit and the leaves form rosettes in mats or cushions. Some species have white lines on their leaves, which adds to their attraction.

CULTIVATION. Grow in well-drained soil in sun or partial shade, although some species will tolerate full sun. Plant autumn or spring. Propagate from seed in spring, by division after flowering or by cuttings summer to autumn.

RECOMMENDED. S. caesia, S. cotyledon, S. crustata, S. x fortunei, S. granulata, S. juniperifolia, S. longifolia, S. marginata, S. moschata, S.m. Cloth of Gold, S. oppositifolia, S. porophylla, S. retus, S. scardica, S. stolonifera, S. umbrosa.

▲ *Saxifraga* x *apiculata*

Saxifraga x Jenkinsae ▼

▼ *Saxifraga* x *fortunei*

▼ *Saxifraga stolonifera* Tricolour

Saxifraga oppositifolia ▼

▲ *Saxifraga juniperifolia* Macedonica

Saxifraga longifolia ▲

▲ *Saxifraga scardica*

Saxifraga marginata ▼

▲ *Saxifraga porophylla*

Saxifraga x urbium ▼

Scabiosa

A genus of 80–100 species of annuals and perennials with a tufted to clump-forming habit. The leaves are accompanied by flower-heads with the same composition as a daisy.

CULTIVATION. Grow in well-drained, fertile soil in sun. Plant perennials autumn to spring; sow annuals *in situ* in spring. Propagate perennials by division autumn or spring,or seed in spring.

RECOMMENDED. S. *atropurpurea*, S. *caucasia*, S.c. Loddon White, S. *columbaria*, S. *graminifolia*, S.g. Pinkushion, S. *lucida*, S. *ochroleuca*.

Scabiosa ochroleuca ▶

Schisandra

A genus of 25 species of woody climbing plants, one of which is most decorative: S. *grandiflora*. The stems have a twining habit and the pointed, toothed leaves are accompanied by bowl-shaped, pale pink, nodding flowers. The fruit is a rounded red berry in dense spikes.

CULTIVATION. Grow in humus-rich soil in sun or partial shade. Plant autumn to spring, providing support for the twining stems. Propagate from seed, by layering in spring or cuttings in summer.

RECOMMENDED. S. *grandiflora*.

◀ *Schisandra grandiflora rubriflora*

Schizanthus

A genus of 10–15 species of annuals, biennials and short-lived perennials from Chile. They have erect stems and 2-lipped, orchid-like flowers.

CULTIVATION. Grow in a well-ventilated, sunny greenhouse or conservatory. May also be grown as a half-hardy annual sown in spring.

RECOMMENDED. S. *pinnatus*, S.p. Dwarf Bouquet, S.p. Giant Hybrid, S.p. Pansy flowered, S. x *wisetonensis*.

Schizanthus pinnatus ▶

Schizophragma

A genus of 4 species of woody stemmed climbers, one species is generally available; *S. hydrangeoides*. The stems cling by aerial roots like those of the ivy. The leaves are sharply toothed and the flowers tiny, 5-petalled and whitish in colour

CULTIVATION. Grow in humus-rich, well-drained soil in sun or partial shade. Effective growing into old trees or over walls. Plant autumn to spring. Propagate from seed, layering in spring or cuttings late summer.

RECOMMENDED. *S. hydrangeoides*, *S.h.* Roseum.

◄ *Schizophragma hydrangeoides*

Schizostylis

A genus 2 species of evergreen, perennials from S. Africa, one is generally available: *S. coccinea*. Also known as the Kaffir lily. A clump or colony-forming species with sword-shaped leaves in fan-like tufts and crimson, crocus-like flowers. Hardy in warm areas, but protect against severe frost.

CULTIVATION. May be grown in a frost-free greenhouse or deep frame for winter-flowering. Plant in humus-rich, moisture retentive soil in sun. Plant and propagate by division in spring.

RECOMMENDED. *S. coccinea*, *S.c.* Mrs Hegarty.

Schizostylis coccinea Major ▶

Scilla

A genus of 80 species of bulbous plants with linear to strap-shaped leaves and 6-petalled, bell to star-shaped flowers.

CULTIVATION. Grow in well-drained, humus-rich soil in sun or partial shade. Half-hardy species best in pots in a frame or greenhouse. Plant or pot in autumn. Propagate from seed, by offsets taken when dormant.

RECOMMENDED. *S. adlamii*, *S. bifolia*, *S. monophylla*, *S. natalensis*, *S. peruviana*. *S.p* Alba, *S. sibirica*, *S.s.* Alba, *S. tubergeniana*, *S. violacea*.

◄ *Scilla tubergeniana*

Sedum

A genus of 500–600 species of succulent perennials and sub-shrubs, including a few annuals and biennials. They have a prostrate to erect habit with succulent leaves accompanied by 5-petalled, starry flowers.

CULTIVATION. Grow hardy species in well-drained soil in sun, half-hardy or tender species under glass. Pot or plant in spring to autumn. Propagate from seed in spring or by stem-cuttings in summer.

RECOMMENDED. *S. caeruleum*, *S. hispanicum*, *S. kamtschaticum*, *S. rosea*, *S. spectabile*, *S. sieboldii*, *S. spathulifolium*, *S. spurium*, *S. telephium*.

▲ *Sedum spurium* Schnorbusser Blut

▲ *Sedum hispanicum*

▲ *Sedum k. ellacombianum*

Sedum sieboldii Medio-variegatum ▼

Sedum spurium ▼

▲ *Sedum spectabile* Autumn Joy

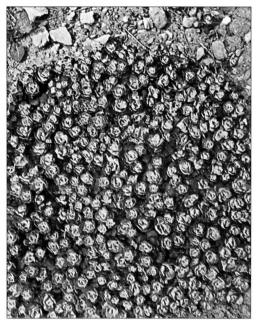

▲ *Sedum spathulifolium* Purpureum

◀ *Sedum s. Cape Blanco*   *Sedum caeruleum* ▼

◀ *Sedum rosea*

Sempervivum

A genus of 25–40 species of perennial succulents. Hummock to mat forming in habit with dense rosettes of fleshy leaves, often tinted red or purple. Each rosette can take several years to flower, but produces offsets annually.

CULTIVATION. Grow in well-drained soil in sun, in screes, rock crevices, dry walls or sink gardens. Plant autumn or spring. Propagate by division at planting time or from offsets in late summer.

RECOMMENDED. *S. allionii, S. arachnoideum, S. ballsii, S. bicolour, S. calcareum, S. ciliosum, S. elegans, S. grandiflorum, S. giuseppii, S. hirtum, S. kosaninii, S. marmoreum, S. nevadense, S. octopodes, S.o. apetalum, S. soboliferum, S. tectorum, S.t. alpinum, S.t. glaucum.*

▲ *Sempervivum grandiflorum*   *S. arachnoideum* ▼

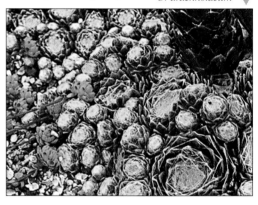

◀ *Sempervivum arachnoideum* in flower

▼ *Sempervivum calcareum*

Sempervivum x Commander Hay ▼

Senecio semperivens

Senecio x hybridus

Senecio

A genus of 2000 species and is the largest genus of flowering plants including annuals, perennials, shrubs, small trees and climbers. A wide variety of forms, but generally daisy-like flower-heads.

CULTIVATION. Grow hardy species in fertile, well-drained soil in sun. Tender, need a frost-free climate and some light shade. Plant hardy perennials and shrubs autumn to spring. Pot greenhouse species in spring. Propagate perennials by division or basal cuttings in spring, shrubs and trees by cuttings in late summer, succulents by cuttings in summer. All species may be grown from seed in spring.

RECOMMENDED. *S. abrotanifolius*, *S. articulatus*, *S. bicolour cineraria*, *S. compactus*, *S. elegans*, *S. grandifolius*, *S. greyi*, *S. heritieri*, *S. laxifolius*, *S. monroi*, *S. reinoldii*, *S. rotundifolius*, *S. tanguticus*, *S. vira-vira*.

Senecio bicolour cineraria

Silene

A genus of 500 species of annuals, perennials and sub-shrubs. Tufted to clump-forming in habit, prostrate or erect. The 5-petalled flowers are tubular.

CULTIVATION. Grow in well-drained, fertile soil in sun. Plant autumn to spring. Propagate by division at planting time, basal cuttings in spring or from seed in spring.

RECOMMENDED. *S. acaulis*, *S.a. elongata*, *S. armeria*, *S. coeli-rosa*, *S. dioica*, *S. maritima*, *S. pendula*, *S.p. Compacta*, *S. schafta*.

Silene acaulis

Skimmia

A genus of 7–9 species of evergreen shrubs with leathery, aromatic leaves when bruised. The fragrant flowers are 4–5 petalled in spring, followed by berry-like fruit.

CULTIVATION. Grow in humus-rich soil in sun or partial shade. Less hardy types should be placed in sheltered positions. Plant autumn or spring. Propagate by cuttings in late summer, layering in spring, or from seed in a cold frame.

RECOMMENDED. *S. japonica, S.j. Fragrans, S.j. Rogersii, S. laureola, S. reevesiana.*

Skimmia laureola ▶

 Skimmia japonica

Solanum

A genus of over 1500 species of annuals, perennials, shrubs and climbers. They have simple leaves and clusters of flowers with spreading lobes and a central, yellow cone. The fruit consists of a rounded berry.

CULTIVATION. Grow in a sheltered, sunny site or a frost-free greenhouse. Any well-drained soil is suitable. Plant half-hardies in spring and propagate by cuttings in summer. Climbers are best pruned back annually.

RECOMMENDED. *S. capsicastrum, S. crispum*.

Solanum capsicastrum

Soldanella

A genus of 10 species of small, evergreen perennials with a clump to mat-forming habit. The dark green, leathery leaves are accompanied by nodding, bell-shaped flowers in spring.

CULTIVATION. Grow in moisture-retentive, well-drained, preferably gritty, humus-rich soil in sun or partial shade, ideally facing north. Plant autumn or spring. Propagate by division or from seed.

RECOMMENDED. *S. alpina, S. carpatica, S. minima, S. montana, S. pindicola, S. villosa*.

Soldanella villosa

Solidago

A genus of 100 species or perennials with a clump-forming habit and simple, narrow leaves. The yellow flowers are tiny. Also known as golden rod.

CULTIVATION. Grow in any moisture-retentive soil in sun, although partial shade is tolerated. Plant autumn to spring. Propagate by division at planting time or from seed in a cold frame.

RECOMMENDED. *S. canadensis, S. virgaurea, S.v.* Brachystachys, *S.v. cambrica*.

 Solidago Crown of Rays

Sorbus

A genus of trees and shrubs with toothed leaves that can colour in winter. The flowers are small, white to cream, 5-petalled and followed by berry-like fruit.

CULTIVATION. Grow in fertile, well-drained soil in sun. Light shade is tolerated. Plant autumn to spring. Propagate from seed, ideally in a cold frame, cultivars by grafting or layering onto the type species, *S. americana* or *S. aucuparia*.

RECOMMENDED. *S. aria, S. aucuparia, S. cashmiriana, S. fennica, S. hybrida, S. scalaris.*

Sorbus aucuparia ▲

 ◀ *Sorbus hybrida*

▼ *Sorbus cashmiriana*

 Sorbus aria ▼

Sparaxis

A genus of 5 species of cormous perennials. Each corm produces a narrow fan of sword-shaped leaves and a taller, wiry stem bearing 6-petalled flowers similar to crocuses. One species is generally available; S. tricolour.

CULTIVATION. Grow outside in well-drained soil in a sunny sheltered border or in pots under glass. Plant late autumn, providing protection in cold areas. Propagate from seed in spring or from separated corms when dormant.

RECOMMENDED. S. tricolour.

◀ *Sparaxis tricolour*

Spiraea

A genus of 100 species of deciduous shrubs with toothed, narrow leaves. The small, 5-petalled flowers are born on current season's growth.

CULTIVATION. Prune out weak stems if strong stems are required. Plant autumn to spring. Propagate by semi-hardwood cuttings late summer, hardwood cuttings late autumn, suckers removed at planting time or by layering in spring.

RECOMMENDED. S. japonica, S.j. Anthony Waterer, S. menziesii, S. prunifolia, S. thunbergii, S. x vanhouttei.

Spiraea japonica Anthony Waterer ▶

Stachys

A genus of 300 species of annuals, perennials and sub-shrubs with an erect to spreading habit. The 2-lipped spikes of flowers are tubular.

CULTIVATION. Grow in well-drained soil in sun. Plant autumn to spring. Propagate by division at planting time, cuttings in spring or late summer or from seed in spring in a cold frame.

RECOMMENDED. S. affinis, S. byzantina, S.b. Silver Carpet, S. grandiflora, S.g. Robusta, S. nivea, S. officinalis, S.o. Rosea.

◀ *Stachys grandiflora*

Staphylea

A genus of 10 species of deciduous shrubs and small trees. The 5-petalled flowers are followed by bladder-like capsules wthat contain hard, polished, nut-like seeds.

CULTIVATION. Plant autumn to spring. Propagate from seed, by layering in spring, softwood cuttings late spring to early summer or semi-hardwood cuttings late summer.

RECOMMENDED. S. colchia, S. holocarpa, S.h. Rosea, S. pinnata.

Staphylea pinnata ▶

Stephanandra

A genus of 4 species of deciduous shrubs related to *spiraea*. The sharply, toothed leaves are accompanied by tiny, 5-petalled, whitish flowers. Grown for its elegant foliage and winter stems.

CULTIVATION. Plant autumn to spring. Propagate by semi-hardwood cuttings late summer, hardwood cuttings late autumn, suckers removed at planting time or by layering in spring. Protect plants in colder areas.

RECOMMENDED. S. incisa, S.i. Crispa, S. tanakae.

◀ *Stephanandra tanakae*

Sternbergia

A genus of 6–8 species of bulbous plants. They have strap-shaped leaves and yellow, 6-petalled flowers similar to crocuses.

CULTIVATION. Grow in well-drained soil in sheltered, sunny sites. Plant late summer, early autumn. Propagate by separated offsets at planting time or from ripe seed.

RECOMMENDED. S. clusiana, S. fischeriana, S. lutea.

Sternbergia clusiana ▶

Stewartia

A genus of 10 species of deciduous shrubs and trees with smooth, attractively flaking bark. The leaves are toothed and often coloured in autumn. The solitary flowers are white and 5-petalled, flat to bowl-shaped, in late summer.

CULTIVATION. Grow in humus-rich, well-drained, neutral to acid soil, in partial shade. Plant autumn to spring. Propagate from seed, by layering in spring or cuttings in late summer.

RECOMMENDED. *S. koreana*, *S. ovata*, *S. pseudo-camellia*, *S. sinensis*.

◀ *Stewartia pseudocamellia*

Stipa

A genus of 150 species of perennial grasses with a tufted to clump-forming habit. Also known as feather grass or needlegrass. The slender, linear leaves resemble waves when the wind blows over them and they are accompanied by one-flowered spikelets.

CULTIVATION. Grow in well-drained soil in sun. Plant autumn to spring. Propagate by division or from seed in spring.

RECOMMENDED. *S. calamagrostis*, *S. gigantea*, *S. pennata*.

Stipa gigantea

Stokesia

A genus of one species of evergreen perennial; *S. laevis*, also known as Stokes' aster. Clump-forming in habit with soft, spiny-toothed basal leaves. The flower-heads are solitary, somewhat cornflower-like, lavender-blue from summer to autumn.

CULTIVATION. Grow in fertile, well-drained soil in sun. Plant autumn to spring. Propagate from seed in a cold frame or by division in spring.

RECOMMENDED. *S. laevis*.

◀ *Stokesia laevis*

Stranvaesia

A genus of 4–5 species of evergreen shrubs and small trees, one of which is readily available; *S. davidiana*. A large shrub with oblong leaves that can turn red in autumn. The 5-petalled flowers can be red or yellow, in summer, depending on the species. Protect tender species from frost.

CULTIVATION. Grow in any well-drained soil in sun or light shade. Plant autumn to spring. Propagate by cuttings with a heel in summer or seed.

RECOMMENDED. *S. davidiana*, *S.d. salicifolia*, *S.d. undulata*, *S.d.u.* Fructuluteo.

Stranvaesia davidiana ▶

Symphoricarpos

A genus of 18 species of deciduous, suckering shrubs. They have slender, twiggy stems, rounded leaves and small, bell-shaped flowers followed by pink or red berries.

CULTIVATION. Grow in any moisture-retentive soil in sun or shade. Plant autumn to spring. Propagate by division or suckers at planting time, cuttings in late summer or autumn from seed.

RECOMMENDED. *S. albus*, *S.* x *chenaultii*, *S.* x *doorenbosii*, *S. orbiculatus*, *S.o.* Variegatus, *S. rivularis*.

◀ *Symphoricarpos rivularis*

Symphytum

A genus of 25 species or perennials with a clump-forming or rhizomatous habit. The leaves can be rough-textured and the flowers tubular to funnel-shaped. An undemanding plant that is happy to grow in a wide variety of conditions.

CULTIVATION. Grow in any reasonably fertile, moisture-retentive soil in sun or partial shade. Plant autumn to spring. Propagate by division at planting time or from seed in spring.

RECOMMENDED. *S. caucasicum*, *S. grandiflorum*, *S. officinale*, *S. rubrum*, *S.* x *uplandicum*.

Symphytum x *uplandicum* Variegatum ▶

Syringa x *prestoniae*

Syringa

A genus of 30 species of deciduous shrubs and small trees. The fragrant flowers are tubular with spreading petals.

CULTIVATION. Grow in fertile, moisture-retentive soil in sun or partial shade. Plant autumn to spring. Propagate by suckers at planting time (not grafted cultivars), layering in spring, cuttings in late summer in a frame or hardwood cuttings outside in autumn.

RECOMMENDED. *S. afghanica, S. emodii, S. microphylla, S. palibiniana, S. reflexa, S. villosa.*

◀ *Syringa vulgaris* Primrose

Syringa x *persica* ▼

Syringa vulgaris Maud Notcutt

Tagetes

A genus of 30–50 species of half-hardy and tender annuals and perennials. The annuals mentioned here are erect, with terminal, bell-shaped flower-heads.

CULTIVATION. Grow in any well-drained, moderately fertile soil in sun. Sow seed in spring. Harden off and plant out when all danger of frost has passed. Seed can also be sown *in situ* in early summer.

RECOMMENDED. *T. erecta, T. minuta, T. patula, T. tenuifolia, T.t. pumila.*

Tagetes erecta Lemon Lady ▶

▼ *Tagetes patula* Gypsy Dancers

Tagetes tenuifolia Orange Gem ▼

Tamarix

A genus of 54 species of deciduous shrubs and small trees. They are slender-stemmed with scale-like, feathery leaves and tiny flowers borne at the ends of the branches. Very tolerant of both drought and strong winds.

CULTIVATION. Grow in well-drained soil in sun. Plant autumn to spring. Propagate by semi-hardwood cuttings in late summer, hardwood cuttings in late autumn or *in situ.*

RECOMMENDED. *T. aestivalis, T. gallica, T. parviflora, T. ramosissima, T. tetrandra.*

Tamarix tetrandra ▶

Tanacetum

A genus of 50 species of annuals and perennials. Closely allied to *chrysanthemum*, and often difficult to distinguish from that genus.

CULTIVATION. Grow in moderately fertile, well-drained soil in sun. Plant autumn to spring. Propagate by division at planting time, from seed and basal cuttings in spring.

RECOMMENDED. *T. argenteum*, *T. densum*, *T. haradjanii*, *T. herderi*, *T. ptarmaciflorum*, *T. vulgare*.

 Tanacetum vulgare

Tecophilaea

A genus of 2 species of cormous-rooted plants from Chile, one species is readily available; *T. cyanocrocus*. The linear leaves are basal, usually only 2–3 with crocus-like flowers, deep gentian-blue with a white eye in spring.

CULTIVATION. Grow in sharply drained, but fertile, soil in sunny sheltered sites, in mild areas ideally at the foot of a south wall. Can be grown in pots. Plant or pot in autumn. Propagate from seed in spring or from offsets removed at potting time.

RECOMMENDED. *T. cyanocrocus*, *T.c. violacea*.

Tecophilaea cyanocrocus

Teucrium

A genus of 300 species of evergreen perennials and shrubs with tubular, 2-lipped flowers.

CULTIVATION. Grow in well-drained soil in sun or for some species, partial shade. Plant autumn to spring. Propagate by division or from seed in spring, or cuttings in summer.

RECOMMENDED. *T. aroanium*, *T. chamaedrys*, *T. fruticans*, *T. marum*, *T. polium*, *T. pyrenaicum*, *T. scorodonia*, *T.s. Crispum*, *T. subspinosum*.

 Teucrium polium

Thalictrum

A genus of 100 species of perennials. They have a clump-forming habit and form colonies. Grown for their lovely, delicate, small, petalless flowers. The foliage is slightly blue-grey in colour.

CULTIVATION. Grow in humus-rich, moisture-retentive, but well-drained, soil in sun or partial shade. Plant autumn to spring. Propagate from seed when ripe in spring or by division at planting time.

RECOMMENDED. *T. aquilegifolium*, *T. delavayi*, *T. diffusiflorum*, *T. glaucum*, *T. kiusianum*, *T. minus.*

Thalictrum aquilegifolium ▶

▼ *Thalictrum flavum glaucum*

Thalictrum dipterocarpum ▼

Thermopsis

A genus of 20–30 species of herbaceous perennials with erect stems bearing lupin-like, yellow or golden-yellow flowers.

CULTIVATION. Grow in fertile, well-drained soil in sun. Plant autumn or spring. Propagate by division when planting or from seed under glass in spring.

RECOMMENDED. *T. caroliniana*, *T. mollis*, *T. montana.*

Thermopsis caroliniana ▶

Thuja

A genus of 5 evergreen trees with a range of cultivar heights from 60 m to 75 cm. They form cone shaped specimens in green to golden yellow colours and can change colour over the winter.

CULTIVATION. Grow in humus-rich soil in sun or shade. Plant autumn or spring. Propagate from seed in spring or cuttings with a heel in late summer.

RECOMMENDED. *T. occidentalis, T. orientalis, T.o.* Rosedalis, *T. plicata, T.p. zebrina.*

◀ *Thuja plicata*

Thuja occidentalis Rosedalis ▼

Thunbergia

A genus of 100 species of annuals and perennials, often climbing. They have erect or twining stems and tubular flowers.

CULTIVATION. Grow in greenhouse borders or pots filled with a good potting mixture. Provide humidity and light shade in summer. Water regularly during the growing season. Pot in spring. Propagate from seed in spring and perennials by cuttings in summer.

RECOMMENDED. *T. alata, T. grandiflora, T. gregorii.*

◀ *Thunbergia alata*

Thymus

A genus of 300 species of shrubs and sub-shrubs. They have wiry, erect to prostrate stems and aromatic leaves. The small, 2-lipped flowers grow in spikes or heads.

CULTIVATION. Grow in any well-drained soil in sun. Plant autumn to spring. Propagate by division, from seed in spring or by cuttings early to late summer.

RECOMMENDED. *T. caespititius, T. carnosus, T. cilicicus, T. doefleri, T. herba-barona, T. lanuginosus, T. praecox, T. richardii, T. vulgaris.*

Thymus praecox ▶

▼ *Thymus* x *citriodorus* Aureus

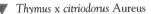

Thymus praecox arcticus Coccineus ▼

Tigridia

A genus of 27 species of bulbous plants from Mexico to Chile, one of which is generally available; *T. pavonia*, also known as the peacock or tiger flower. The pleated, leaves are in fan-like tufts. The flowers have a bowl-shaped base with spreading petals in late summer to autumn.

CULTIVATION. Grow in fertile, well-drained soil in sunny, sheltered sites. Plant in spring, lifting and storing in cold areas over winter. Propagate from seed or by offsets.

RECOMMENDED. *T. pavonia.*

Tigridia pavonia ▶

Torenia

A genus of 40–50 species of annuals and perennials. One species is usually available; *T. fournieri*, also known as blue wings or the wishbone flower. A bushy, erect annual with narrow leaves and tubular flowers in pale violet to blue in summer to autumn.

CULTIVATION. Grow in greenhouse or as a half-hardy annual in fertile, moisture-retentive soil in a sheltered, partial shade. Sow seed in spring.

RECOMMENDED. *T. fournieri*, *T.f.* Grandiflora.

 Torenia fournieri

Trachelium

A genus of 7 species of woody-based perennials from the Mediterranean. The plants have small, slender, tubular, 5-lobed flowers.

CULTIVATION. Grow in sharply drained, fertile soil in sunny,sheltered sites. Not reliably hardy, often grown as a pot plant or as a half-hardy annual. Plant or pot in spring. Propagate from seed in spring or basal cuttings late spring.

RECOMMENDED. *T. caeruleum*, *T. jacquinii rumelianum*.

Trachelium caeruleum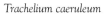

Trachelospermum

A genus of 10–30 species of woody, evergreen climbers with twining stems, some with aerial-clinging roots. The leathery leaves are accompanied by tubular, fragrant, jasmine-like flowers in summer.

CULTIVATION. Grow in humus-rich, moisture-retentive, well-drained soil at the foot of a sunny wall. In cold areas they are best in a frost-free greenhouse. Plant autumn to spring. Propagate by layering in spring or cuttings late summer.

RECOMMENDED. *T. asiaticum*, *T. jasminoides*.

Trachelospermum jasminoides

Tradescantia

A genus of 20–60 species that range from erect, hardy, herbaceous perennials to tender or trailing evergreens. The leaves are somewhat fleshy and the 3-petalled flowers have bearded stamens.

CULTIVATION. Grow hardy species in fertile, well-drained, moisture-retentive soil in sun or partial shade. Plant autumn to spring. Propagate by division or from seed in spring.

RECOMMENDED. *T.* x *andersoniana*, *T.* x *a.* Osprey, *T.* x *a.* Purple Dome, *T.* x *a.* Rubra, *T. blossfeldiana*, *T. virginiana*.

Tradescantia x *andersoniana* Osprey ▶

Trillium

A genus of 30 species of herbaceous perennials. They form small to large clumps, with oval leaves and solitary, 3-petalled flowers in spring to early summer. These are followed by a reddish berry.

CULTIVATION. Grow in moisture-retentive, well-drained, humus-rich soil in partial shade. Plant when dormant. Propagate by division at planting time or from ripe seed.

RECOMMENDED. *T. californicum*, *T. chloropetalum*, *T.c. giganteum*, *T. erectum*, *T. grandiflorum*, *T. nivale*, *T. ovatum*, *T. recurvatum*, *T. sessile*.

◀ *Trillium grandiflorum*

Tripteris

A genus of 40 species of annuals and perennials, one of which is usually available; *T. hyoseroides*. A bushy, erect, aromatic annual with slender stems and narrow, toothed leaves. The flower-heads are daisy-like, with blue-black discs and brilliant, yellow-orange petals in summer to autumn.

CULTIVATION. Grow in fertile, well-drained soil in sun. Sow seed *in situ* late spring or when all danger of frost has passed.

RECOMMENDED. *T. hyoseroides*.

Tripteris hyoseroides ▶

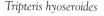

Trollius

A genus of 20–25 species of herbaceous perennials with a clump-forming habit and long-stalked leaves. The flowers are like large buttercups, but more rounded and formed of 5–15 yellow petals.

CULTIVATION. Grow in fertile, moist soil or preferably a bog garden in sun, although partial shade is tolerated. Propagate by division at planting time or from seed sown when ripe.

RECOMMENDED. *T. acaulis, T. europaeus, T. ledebourii, T. yunnanensis.*

◀ *Trollius yunnanensis*

Tropaeolum

A genus of 50–90 species of annual and perennial climbers and trailers. Often tuberous-rooted, the leaves produce long stalks that act as tendrils supporting the plant. Each bloom has spreading petals that are followed by fruit.

CULTIVATION. Grow tender species under glass, hardy perennials in humus-rich, well-drained soil in sun. Annuals will grow in any soil in sun.

RECOMMENDED. *T.* Burpeei, *T. majus, T. peltophorum, T. peregrinum, T. polyphyllum, T. speciosum, T. tricolourum, T. tuberosum.*

Tropaeolum Dwarf Double Jewel

▼ *Tropaeolum majus* Alaska

Tropaeolum peregrinum ▼

Tulipa

A genus of 50–150 species of bulbous plants. Each plant consists of an erect stem bearing a few linear leaves and a terminal, usually erect, 6-petalled, cup-shaped flower per stem. Flowers can be single or double depending on species grown. Fruit is a large capsule with disc-like seed. Each bulb is of annual duration, new ones are formed at the base of the stem each year.

CULTIVATION. Grow in any moderately fertile, well-drained soil in sun. Plant mid to late autumn, ideally lifting and replanting annually. Propagate from offsets when replanting or from seed in a cold frame. Both species and cultivars make good pot plants for the cold greenhouse or home. Specially-treated bulbs of cultivars for forcing will stand warmer conditions than those for narcissi.

RECOMMENDED. Species: *T. acuminata*, *T. aitchisonii*, *T. batalini*, *T. fosteriana*, *T. gesneriana*, *T. greigii*, *T. hageri*, *T. humilis*, *T. kaufmanniana*, *T. linifolia*, *T. praestans*, *T. saxatilis*, *T. sylvestris*, *T. tarda*, *T. turkestanica*, *T. whittallii*. Cultivars: *T.* Aladdin, *T.* Apeldoorn, *T,* Dutch Princess, *T.* Golden Harvest, *T.* May Blossom, *T.* Mount Tacoma, *T.* Oriental Splendour, *T.* Purissima, *T.* Texas Gold, *T.* The Bishop, *T.* The First.

▲ *Tulipa saxatilis*

Tulipa Oriental Splendour ▶

▼ *Tulipa* May Blossom

Tulipa Dutch Princess ▶

▼ *Tulipa* Appledoorn   ▲ *Tulipa* Golden Harvest   *Tulipa* Aladdin ▼

▼ *Tulipa* Texas Gold   *Tulipa* The Bishop ▼

Ulex

A genus of 20 species of densely spiny shrubs, one of which is grown in gardens; U. *europaeus*, also known as gorse. Bushy in habit, the stems and shoots are spine-tipped. The flowers are pea-shaped, bright yellow, fragrant and bloom in spring and summer, but can flower in mild winters.

CULTIVATION. Grow in well-drained, sandy or chalky soil in full sun. Plant autumn to spring. Propagate from seed in spring, *in situ* or in small pots to avoid root damage at transplanting time.

RECOMMENDED. U. *europaeus*.

Ulex europaeus ▶

Uvularia

A genus of 4–5 species of herbaceous perennials that eventually grow to form colonies of erect to arching stems. The pendant, 6-petalled flowers are bell-like and pale to lemon yellow in colour.

CULTIVATION. Grow in moisture-retentive, but not wet, humus-rich soil in partial shade. Plant autumn to early spring. Propagate by division at planting time or from seed.

RECOMMENDED. U. *grandiflora*, U. *perfoliata*.

◀ *Uvularia grandiflora*

Vaccinium

A genus of 100–400 species of evergreen and deciduous shrubs. They have nodding, bell to urn-shaped flowers and edible, fleshy, berry-fruit.

CULTIVATION. Grow in acid, preferably peaty soil, well-drained, but moist, in sun or partial shade. Plant autumn or spring. Propagate by division, rooted suckers or cuttings with a heel in late summer or early autumn.

RECOMMENDED. V. *angustifolium*, V. *corymbosum*, V.c. Early Blue, V. *delavayi*, V. *floribundum*, V. *moupinense*, V. *nummularia*, V. *vitis-idaea*.

Vaccinium nummularia ▶

Venidium

A genus of 20–30 species of half-hardy perennials and annuals, one of which is usually available; *V. fastuosum*. They have grey, hairy leaves and golden-yellow to bright orange flowers with a brown basal blotch in summer to autumn, only opening in sun.

CULTIVATION. Grow in fertile soil in sun. Sow seed under glass in spring, hardening off and planting out only when all danger of frost has passed.

RECOMMENDED. *V. fastuosum*, *V.f.* Art Shades.

◀ *Venidium fastuosum*

Verbascum

A genus of 200–350 species of biennials, perennials and sub-shrubs. The perennials and biennials are rosette-forming, the latter into clumps and with hairy leaves and long spikes of flowers. The sub-shrubs are twiggy.

CULTIVATION. Grow in well-drained soil in sun. Propagate all species from seed in spring, perennials by division and sub-shrubs, by cuttings of roots late summer. Biennials can be sown *in situ*.

RECOMMENDED. *V. arctus*, *V. chaixii*, *V. densiflorum*, *V. dumulosum*, *V. phoeniceum*, *V. vernale*.

Verbascum phoeniceum Gainsborough ▶

Verbena

A genus of 250 species of annuals, perennials and shrubs with an erect to prostrate habit. The leaves are linear, toothed and accompanied by small, 2-lipped, tubular flowers.

CULTIVATION. Grow in fertile, well-drained soil in sun. Half-hardy types should be planted out only when all frost has passed and over-wintered under glass. Plant hardy species in spring. Propagate from seed in spring under glass, hardy species also by division; all species by cuttings.

RECOMMENDED. *V. peruviana*, *V. rigida*, *V. tenera*.

◀ *Verbena tenera* Mahonettii

Veronica

A genus of 300 annuals and perennials, also known as speedwell. A quick growing species that is clump-forming. The linear leaves are accompanied by blue spikes of irregular flowers. The blues vary from pale sky-blue to deep indigo.

CULTIVATION. Grow in fertile, well-drained soil in sun. Plant autumn to spring. Propagate by division at planting time or from seed in spring, evergreen perennials by cuttings in summer.

RECOMMENDED. *V. austriaca, V. cinerea, V. fruticans, V. pectinata, V. selleri, V. spicata, V. virginica.*

Veronica austriaca teucrium Trehane ▶

Viburnum

A genus of 200 species of evergreen and deciduous shrubs. They have terminal, often flattish, clusters of small, tubular, mainly white flowers, followed by berry-like fruits.

CULTIVATION. Grow the hardy species in fertile. well-drained soil in sun or partial shade. Plant autumn to spring. Propagate from seed, by layering in late winter or cuttings in late summer.

RECOMMENDED. *V. carlesii, V. lantana, V. plicatum, V. opulus, V. rhytidophylloides, V. tinus.*

◀ *Viburnum lantana*

Viburnum tinus ▼

Viola

A genus of 500 species of annuals and perennials that are mostly clump-forming with linear leaves. Some species are semi-climbers whilst others mimic house leeks. The flowers are either horizontally borne or nodding and have 5 petals. Many species produce flowers that never open and also produce seed by self-fertilization. Commonly known in the garden as pansies.

CULTIVATION. Grow in moderately humus-rich, well-drained soil in partial shade or sun. Plant autumn to spring. Propagate from seed, by division in spring or by basal cuttings late summer in a cold frame. For winter and spring-flowering pansies, sow seed late summer in nursery rows or boxes and plant out the young plants into permanent sites in late autumn. For summer blooming, sow seed under glass in early spring, then set out plants, late spring.

RECOMMENDED. Species: *V. aetolica, V. cornuta,* V.c. Alba, *V. cucculata, V. gracilis, V. hederacea, V. labradorica,* V.l. *purpurea, V. lyallii, V. odorata, V. riviniana, V. rupestris, V. septentrionalis, V. sororia,* V.s. *Albiflora, V. tricolour, V. verecunda yakusimana.* Cultivars: *V.* x *williamsii, V.* x *w.* Norah Leigh, *V.* x *w.* Norah, *V.* x *w.* White Swan, *V.* x *wittrockiana, V.* x *w.* Celestial Sun, *V.* x *w.* Winter Sun.

▼ *Viola* x *williamsii* Blue Heaven

▲ *Viola x wittrockiana*

Viola x wittrockiana Monch ▲

▲ *Viola cornuta* Alba

▲ *Viola x wittrockiana* Jungfrau

Viola x wittrockiana Arkwright ▼

Viola x wittrockiana Gemini ▼

Waldsteinia

A genus of 5–6 species of mat-forming perennials, one of which is generally available; *W. ternata.* An evergreen species with irregularly toothed leaves and flowers in stalked clusters of 2–7 petals, yellow and blooming in spring to early summer. A good ground cover plant for sunny or shaded areas.

CULTIVATION. Grow in any well-drained soil. Plant autumn to spring. Propagate by division at planting time.

RECOMMENDED. *W. ternata.*

Waldsteinia ternata ▶

Watsonia

A genus of 60–70 species of cormous perennials with a clump-forming habit. Each corm produces a fan of sword-shaped leaves and a slender spike of flowers.

CULTIVATION. Grow in fertile, well-drained soil in sun. Species below are half-hardy and will need protection in winter. Plant or pot in spring. Propagate by division, or from seed, growing on in pots for the first year.

RECOMMENDED. *W. ardernii, W. marginata, W. versfeldii.*

◀ *Watsonia ardernii*

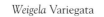

Weigela

A genus of 10–12 species of deciduous shrubs with small, clusters of funnel-shaped, 5-lobed flowers in early summer.

CULTIVATION. Grow in fertile soil, preferably in sun, although partial shade is tolerated. Plant autumn to spring. Propagation by semi-hardwood cuttings late summer, hardwood cuttings outside in autumn or from seed in spring.

RECOMMENDED. *W.* Avalanche, *W. floribunda, W. florida, W. middendorffiana, W.* Newport Red, *W.* Variegata.

Weigela Variegata ▶

Wisteria

A genus of 9–10 species of beautiful, woody climbers and an easy specimen to grow. The fragrant, pendant pea-flowers are spectacular when covering a pergola or small tree. These are followed by large, bean-shaped pods that explode when ripe.

CULTIVATION. Grow in humus-rich, well-drained, moisture-retentive soil in sun. Provide support for twining stems. Plant autumn or spring. Propagate from seed under glass, layering in spring or cuttings late summer. Pruning is important to achieve good flowers. Cut back new growth each summer and again in winter.

RECOMMENDED. *W. floribunda*, *W.f.* Alba, *W. sinensis*, *W.s.* Alba, *W.s.* Black Dragon, *W.s.* Plena.

Wisteria sinensis ▲

◀ *Wisteria floribunda* Macrobotrys

Yucca

A genus of 40 species of evergreen trees and shrubs. They can be stemless or have erect, robust, stems bearing rosettes of linear, pointed leaves and large bell-shaped, white to cream flowers.

CULTIVATION. Grow hardy species in well-drained soil in sunny, sheltered sites. Plant autumn to spring. Propagate from seed under glass or by separating suckers in spring.

RECOMMENDED. *Y. filamentosa*, *Y. flaccida*, *Y. glauca*, *Y. gloriosa*, *Y. recurvifolia*, *Y. smalliana*.

Yucca filamentosa Variegata ▶

Zantedeschia

A genus of 6 species of perennials with short, thick, fleshy, rhizomes and tufts of long-stalked leaves. The small, petalless flowers are showy in summer.

CULTIVATION. Grow in greenhouse conditions. Pot early in spring. Propagate by offsets separated at potting time or from seed in spring.

RECOMMENDED. Z. *aethiopica*, Z.a. Crowborough, Z. *albomaculata*, Z. *elliottiana*, Z. *rehannii*.

 Zantedeschia aethiopica

Zauschneria

A genus of 4 species of a woody-based perennials. They have linear to ovate leaves and terminal clusters of tubular, fuschia-like flowers.

CULTIVATION. Grow in well-drained soil in sunny, sheltered sites. Plant autumn or spring. Propagate by cuttings of non-flowering shoots in late summer or by division in spring. In cold areas provide protection.

RECOMMENDED. Z. *californica*, Z.c. *canescens*, Z.c. *latifolia*, Z. *cana*.

Zauschneria cana

Zenobia

A genus of one species of semi-evergreen shrub; Z. *pulverulenta*. The leaves are toothed, bright and waxy when young. The fragrant, bell-shaped flowers are waxy-white in pendulous umbels in summer.

CULTIVATION. Grow in moisture-retentive, peaty, acid soil, preferably in partial shade. Plant autumn to spring. Propagate from seed or by layering in spring, by cuttings late summer and suckers at planting time.

RECOMMENDED. Z. *pulverulenta*, Z.p. *nitida*.

Zenobia pulverulenta

Zephyranthes

A genus of 40 species of bulbous perennials with tufts of evergreen or deciduous leaves and solitary, tubular-based flowers.

CULTIVATION. Grow hardy or half-hardy species in well-drained, moderately fertile soil in sunny, sheltered sites, protecting the half-hardies in cold areas. Propagate by separating offsets, dividing clumps at planting time or from seed in spring.

RECOMMENDED. Z. *candida*, Z. *citrina*, Z. *grandiflora*, Z. *tubispatha*.

Zephyranthes grandiflora

Zigadenus

A genus of 15 species of bulbous or rhizomatous perennials mainly from North America, one of which is generally available; Z. *elegans*. A clump-forming species with linear leaves and 6-petalled, greenish-white flowers.

CULTIVATION. Grow in moisture-retentive, but not wet, neutral to acid, preferably peaty soil. Plant autumn to spring. Propagate by division or seed in spring.

RECOMMENDED. Z. *elegans*.

◀ *Zigadenus elegans*

Zinnia

A genus of 17–20 species of annuals, perennials and shrubs. They have a mainly erect habit with large, solitary flower-heads in a range of warm colours. Flowers bloom from mid-summer until the first frosts. A good, cut flower species, smelling of beeswax.

CULTIVATION. Grow in humus-rich soil in full sun and sheltered from strong winds. Sow seed in spring. Plant out late spring.

RECOMMENDED. Z. *elegans*, Z.*e*. State Fair, Z.*e*. Super Giants, Z. *haageana*, Z.*h*. Old Mexico.

Zinnia elegans Scarlet Ruffles